MW01407148

JAMES

FOR PRETEEN AND TEEN GIRLS

FOLLOWING GOD'S Road Signs

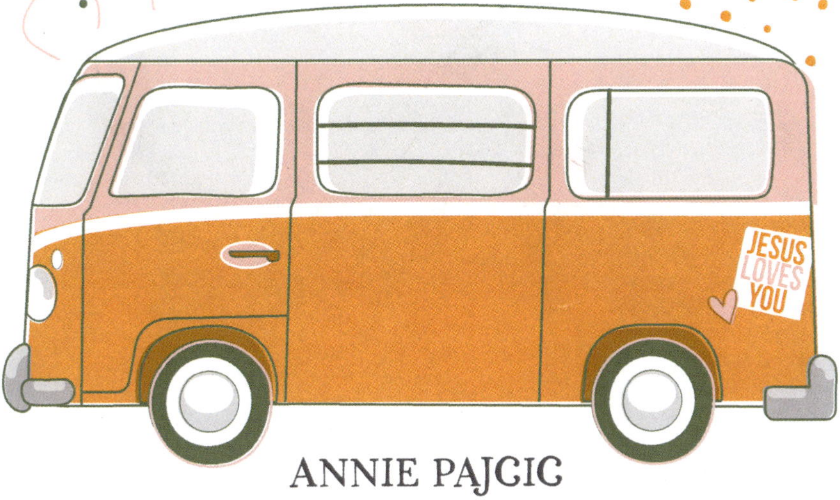

ANNIE PAJCIC

THOUARTEXALTED, INC.

Creating Art through God's Word
www.thouartexalted.com

JAMES: Following God's Road Signs • For Preteen and Teen Girls
Copyright © 2020 by Annie Pajcic
All rights reserved.

ISBN-978-0-9896141-9-1

Scripture quotations came from the following sources:

Unless otherwise stated, all Scripture quotations are taken from the THE HOLY BIBLE, NEW INTERNATIONAL VERSION (NIV)®. Copyright © 1973, 1978, 1984, 2011 by Biblica, Inc.™ Used by permission. All rights reserved worldwide.

Scripture from The International Children's Bible (ICB)®. Copyright © 1986, 1988, 1999 by Thomas Nelson, Inc. Used by permission. All rights reserved.

Scripture taken from The Message (MSG)®. Copyright © 1993, 1994, 1995, 1996, 2000, 2001, 2002. Used by permission of NavPress Publishing Group.

The NEW AMERICAN STANDARD BIBLE (NASB)®. Copyright© 1960,1962,1963,1968,1971, 1960,1962,1963,1968,1971,1972,1973,1975,1977,1995 by The Lockman Foundation. Used by permission.

Scripture taken from THE Holy Bible, New Living Translation (NLT)®. Copyright © 1996, 2004, 2007 by Tyndale House Foundation. Used by permission of Tyndale House Publishers, Inc., Carol Stream, Illinois 60188. All rights reserved.

Dictionary definitions are from www.freedictionary.com and www.blueletterbible.com

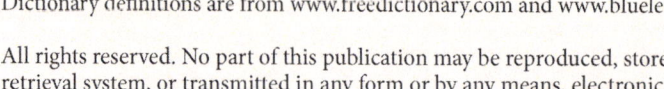

All rights reserved. No part of this publication may be reproduced, stored in a retrieval system, or transmitted in any form or by any means, electronic, mechanical, photocopying, recording, or otherwise, without the prior permission of the Publisher.

Art Direction, Interior Composition, and Design by Annie Pajcic and Rachel Hamner.
Published by Annie Pajcic Design, Jacksonville, Florida.

www.thouartexalted.com

TABLE OF CONTENTS

Welcome and How to Use This Study 4
Art Projects and Note From Annie 5

Lessons

James 1:1	First Impressions	6
James 1:2-4	No Parking in Self-Pity	10
James 1:5-8	Stop and Ask for Directions	14
James 1:9-12	Handicapped Thinking, $250 Fine	18
James 1:13-15	Apply the Brakes!	22
James 1:16-18	Red Light, Green Light	26
James 1:19-21	Buckle Up-It Will Save Your Life	30
James 1:22-25	God's GPS	34
James 1:26-27	Walk the Talk	38
ARTIST WORKSHOP: JOY JAR		**42**
James 2:1-4	Stop the Pollution	44
James 2:5-8	Lifetime Warranty, Guaranteed	48
James 2:9-13	No Traffic Violation	52
James 2:14-18	A Porsche with No Power	56
James 2:19-24	Where the Rubber Meets the Road	60
James 2:25-26	No Matter the Make or Model	64
ARTIST WORKSHOP: HEART ART		**68**
James 3:1-6	Cool Down the Radiator	70
James 3:7-12	No Diesel Fuel in an Unleaded Engine	74
James 3:13-18	The Divine Driver's Manual	78
ARTIST WORKSHOP: FAITH BANNER		**82**
James 4:1-3	A Closer Look Under the Hood of Earthly Wisdom	84
James 4:4-6	Stop, Right Turn Only	88
James 4:7-10	Yield	92
James 4:11-17	Dead End or New Beginning?	96
ARTIST WORKSHOP: WISE OLE' OWL PILLOW		**100**
James 5:1-6	Behave Behind the Wheel	102
James 5:7-11	10-Minute Oil Change	106
James 5:12-16	Clean Our Your Car!	110
James 5:17-20	U-Turn Ahead	114
ARTIST WORKSHOP: THE HOUSE OF GOD		**118**
James 1-5	The Road of Review	120
ADDITIONAL ARTIST WORKSHOP: THE JAMES JOURNAL		**124**

WELCOME TO JAMES!

James: Following God's Road Signs is a 27-lesson Bible study on the book of James for Middle and High school girls. It is written to encourage, guide, and deepen faith when girls hit the bumpy roads in life. But there is good news! God is on our side and gives us INSTRUCTIONS for how to navigate—even when we choose to drive our own way often finding ourselves on a dead-end street. The book of James is a road map guiding us in the right direction.

Following God's Road Signs teaches girls to put their FAITH INTO ACTION by stopping, looking at God's map, and asking Him for directions. This study is great for youth groups, small groups, homeschool groups, or personal study.

HOW TO USE THIS STUDY

This creative Bible study takes you through the book of James chapter by chapter and word by word. Using the connection with **"Following God's Road Signs,"** we will drive slow and stop often. God wants us to take time to learn His ways. It's easy to get distracted, but God wants you to keep your eyes on the road and focus on His Word.

Each lesson highlights:

>**Scripture:** We will be reading through the entire book of James word for word over 27-lessons.
>**Definition:** Each lesson has a definition that identifies a theme for that specific passage of Scripture.
>**Discussion:** Using the definition as a foundational point, we will discuss the passage and dive deeper into a scripted scenario that girls might experience today.
>**Directional Questions:** Four questions for girls to take the Scripture passage and apply it "real time" into their lives.
>**Backroad Drivin':** A summation of the Scripture passage.
>**Additional Sightseeing:** Extra passages to look up to dig further into God's Word.
>**Stop and Write Down Your Prayers:** A prayer and journal section to write notes and add prayers.

Examples of lessons include:

* No Parking in Self Pity/ James 1:2-4
* Stop and Ask for Directions/ James 1:5-8
* No Traffic Violation/ James 2:9-13
* The Divine Driver's Manual/ James 3:13-18
* Dead End or New Beginning/ James 4:11-17
* Behave Behind the Wheel/ James 5:1-6

ART PROJECTS

James, Following God's Road Signs offers **five art projects** with one bonus project that reinforce each chapter. Each art project is fun, easy, and comes with an art instructional video that can be found on our website. ThouArtExalted is a creative ministry that partners with art to reinforce Scripture. It's an excellent learning tool and will help to remind you the directions God wants you to go!

Each art project video can be found on
thouartexalted.com/James-art
The password is: GREEN LIGHT

I am beyond excited you have joined me on this journey to study the book of James and to **Follow God's Road Signs.** Navigating middle and high school can be tough and these years often take you on turns you aren't expecting. Thankfully, this study will provide you with God's road map that will lead you in the right direction.

Whoo hoo! Here we go! I am praying for YOU and your journey to keep your eyes on Jesus. Please reach out if you have any questions, prayers, or need art support. Just email me at annie@thouartexalted.com.

GOD SPEED and safe driving,

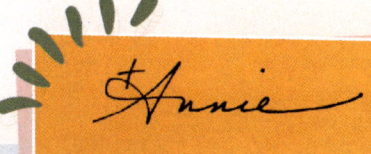

JAMES 1:1 — FIRST IMPRESSIONS

"From James, a servant of God and of the Lord Jesus Christ. To all of God's people who are scattered everywhere in the world: **Greetings.**" (ICB)

DEFINITION: Greetings

1. The act or an instance of welcoming or saluting on meeting
a. An expression of friendly salutation

DISCUSSION

When you introduce yourself, what is first thing you want someone to know about you? It's the GOOD things, right? Maybe you're in a new school, running for student council, or going on a youth trip where you do not know ANYONE. Your natural desire is to make a good FIRST IMPRESSION.

Did you know that James was the half-brother of Jesus? Yet, James fails to mention this to us in the introduction. Don't you think this would have been an **important** piece of information to include as the author of this book? Being blood related to Jesus is **GOOD** first impression material.

James is teaching us a valuable life-long lesson. Instead of boasting about his blood line, James introduces himself as a "servant of God and of the Lord Jesus"—FIRST.
Would you introduce yourself as a servant of God even BEFORE all the good things you have accomplished? Even before the sports you play, the grades you make, where your family lives, who your friends are, and that your aunt rode down the elevator with Justin Beiber?

James teaches us that BEFORE we say, "GREETINGS," we must know WHOSE we are, before we introduce WHO we are.

DIRECTIONAL QUESTIONS

1. How many different ways can you say, "GREETINGS?" (Be creative! Think of different cultures and personalities.)

2. When you introduce yourself, what are three things you want someone to know about you? What are the three things you like best about yourself?

3. The book of James was written to Christians everywhere to show believers how to practice their faith. With this information, why would James introduce himself as a servant of the Lord Jesus Christ and not His half-brother?

4. **JAMES: Following God's Road Signs** is a Bible study on directional "God-signs" that lead us through faith in Jesus. How is knowing you are a servant of Jesus following His Road Signs?

"KNOW **WHOSE** YOU ARE BEFORE YOU INTRODUCE **WHO** YOU ARE".

BACKROAD DRIVIN'

James wrote this letter to ALL believers in Christ scattered abroad. This includes YOU and ME! James' letter to us is about taking our FAITH into ACTION. God gives us great directions to map our way through life. But, He also gives us CHOICES. We can either choose the world's road signs leading to U-turns and dead ends, or we can choose to follow God's perfect map. Let's stop often and ask for His directions. Getting lost is NOT an option.

ADDITIONAL SIGHTSEEING

Look up Ephesians 1:4, John 1:12, and 2 Chronicles 7:14

Identify the three C's of **whose** you are. Ask yourself why these are important when seeing yourself as a servant of God, first. (Answers on bottom)

Ephesians 1:4

John 1:12

2 Chronicles 7:14

I am a CHILD of God, I am CHOSEN by God, and I have been CALLED by God.

STOP and write down your prayers.

Lord,

I represent YOU first! Thank You for the gifts and talents You have given to me. I pray to always glorify YOU and be Your servant, first. Help me to follow YOUR road signs in life. Keep me from U-turns and dead ends. I pray that my FAITH will always be put into action.

Amen.

JAMES 1:1

JAMES 1:2-4
NO PARKING IN SELF-PITY

"Consider it pure **JOY** my brothers, whenever you face trials of many kinds, because you KNOW that the testing of your faith develops **perseverance.** Perseverance must finish its work so that you may be mature and complete, not lacking anything."

DEFINITION: Perseverance

1. continued effort, steady persistence to do something despite difficulties, failure, opposition, or discouragement

DISCUSSION

Consider it JOY when trouble comes your way? Is James clued into the world of girls? Why should I be joyful when I am not happy? These are questions we all ask ourselves, especially when we've have had a day like this one.

My headache started in math class when Ms. Meyer sprang a pop-quiz. The whole class got an A, except me. At lunch, I spilled yogurt on my new skirt (Mom's NOT going to be happy) and then I managed to skin my knee doing a "not-so" graceful fall down the brick steps of the cafeteria. I can't seem to find a friend since I moved to this new school, and who is going to like a yogurt smelling, leg bleeding, math drop-out like me?

STOP! If this situation sounds familiar, you need to take a serious **U-TURN!** Parking here in self-pity will only buy you a ticket to misery. God understands your tough days, but He also wants to build your character through them. Counting it ALL JOY, especially when hard things happen, is a crazy change to our normal way of thinking. We tend to focus only on ourselves when we are challenged by trials. God wants to shift our FOCUS off of the situation and onto HIM. Why? Because He

KNOWS our personal trials expose our faith—what we REALLY believe in. He allows trials in our life to build our confidence and trust in Him.

Trusting in God when life is easy, is . . . EASY. But when life gets hard, **U-TURN YOUR EYES on HIM.** He is building your FAITH so that you will be mature and complete. Don't STOP! Persevere. Keep going despite all the bumps in the road . . . or stains on your skirt.

DIRECTIONAL QUESTIONS

1. What trials are you experiencing right now?

2. Trials aren't easy. How can you choose to be **joyful** in the middle of them?

3. When trials "of many kinds" hit your life, where is your FOCUS? Why does self-pity raise its ugly head? How can you focus on God trusting that He is building your confidence in Him?

4. Looking back, when have you persevered during a trial and become more mature in your faith?

"God understands your tough days, but He also wants to build your character through them."

BACKROAD DRIVIN'

HAVE you ever been sick and decided not to finish your medicine because you were feeling better? What happened? Chances are, you got sick again. Medicine, just like **perseverance**, needs **to finish** its work so you can be healthy again. When you are faced with trials, do not park in self-pity. Keep your FOCUS on God, be patient, and don't stop taking the medicine of **perseverance.** Your effort to keep going, despite opposition, will finish its work to make you more mature and complete in your faith!

ADDITIONAL SIGHTSEEING

Look up Jeremiah 29:11, 1 Corinthians 10:13, and 2 Corinthians 1:3,4

What can you KNOW about your faith during times of trial? Identify three things from these verses. (Answers on bottom)

Jeremiah 29:11

1 Corinthians 1:3

2 Corinthians 1:3

I KNOW that: 1. God is faithful and has a plan for me. 2. He will never give me more than I can handle. 3. I can comfort others because of my trials.

STOP
and write down your prayers.

Lord,

Thank You for the trials in my life. I pray to **count it all joy** when I go through difficult situations. I pray to KNOW Your truth and FOCUS on You and not my circumstances. You have a plan for me and **it is good.** Help me to see You in my times of testing and persevere as I grow in my faith and TRUST in You.

Amen.

JAMES 1:2-4

JAMES 1:5-8
STOP AND ASK FOR DIRECTIONS

"If any of you lacks **wisdom**, you should ask God, who gives generously to all without finding fault, and it will be given to you. But when you ask you must **believe** and not doubt, because the one who doubts is like a wave of the sea, blown and tossed by the wind. That person should not expect to receive anything from the Lord. Such a person is double-minded and unstable in all they do."

DEFINITION: Wisdom

1. The ability to discern or judge what is true, right; insight
2. Common sense; good judgment

DISCUSSION

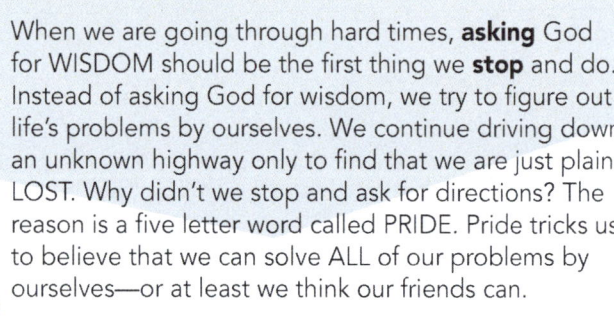

When we are going through hard times, **asking** God for WISDOM should be the first thing we **stop** and do. Instead of asking God for wisdom, we try to figure out life's problems by ourselves. We continue driving down an unknown highway only to find that we are just plain LOST. Why didn't we stop and ask for directions? The reason is a five letter word called PRIDE. Pride tricks us to believe that we can solve ALL of our problems by ourselves—or at least we think our friends can.

Maggie was so stressed she could feel her stomach starting to hurt again. Feeling the pressure of school work, student council, cross country, piano, AND helping her Mom out with her little sister, Maggie felt completely overwhelmed. She picked up her phone to text her best friend when she remembered something she learned at youth group last Sunday. **Stop and ASK God for WISDOM.** *This didn't really work the last time, but then again, she didn't believe God cared about something as small as helping her with Algebra. But something was different. This time, she DID believe that God would help and that He would hear her when she prayed.*

Maggie stopped, took a deep breath, and asked God to help her balance ALL of life's responsibilities. She felt an instant relief of her burdens and to her surprise, when she got home, her little sister was napping. "Thank You, Lord," Maggie said out loud, "A little time to myself. You really do hear my prayers!"

DIRECTIONAL QUESTIONS

1. Without looking, what is the definition of wisdom? When you go through hard times, why should you ask God for wisdom, first? (James 1:5-8)

2. Do you believe God hears you when you pray? (Be honest.) What is the difference between believing and doubting?

3. What do you think being double-minded means? Why is doubting similar to a wave of the sea? Why would God not honor this type of faith?

4. When have you stopped and asked God for wisdom? Looking back, did that situation work out for good and strengthen your faith?

MY WAY OR THE HIGHWAY: TRUE OR FALSE?

BACKROAD DRIVIN'

Have you ever believed that God is too BIG to care about the small things you are going through? On the contrary, God loves you more than you could ever imagine. He would stop heaven to HELP you get back on the right road. You just have to ASK for wisdom and stop doubting like a wave tossed by the sea. Getting lost is super easy when you drive your own route. From your perspective, you can only see a few feet ahead, but God can see the whole map. Focus on Him. He knows the BEST direction for your life and desires to get you home safely.

ADDITIONAL SIGHTSEEING

Look up Proverbs 12:18, Proverbs 16:16, Ecclesiastes 8:1, and 1 Corinthians 1:30

What does the Bible say about WISDOM? Identify four things from these verses. (Answers on bottom)

Proverbs 12:18

_____

_____

Proverbs 16:16

_____

_____

Ecclesiastes 8:1

_____

_____

1 Corinthians 1:30

_____

_____

WISDOM: 1. brings healing. 2. is better than gold or silver (material things). 3. brightens a man's face. 4. In Jesus, we have the wisdom of God.

STOP and write down your prayers.

Lord,

Thank You for Your wisdom. I pray to STOP and ASK for Your directions in my life. I can mess it up pretty quickly when I try to do it my way. Thank You that You understand me. Lead me into truth and help me to discern what is right. Help me to ALWAYS believe in You and not doubt. You are the only One who knows the right way.

Amen.

James 1:5-8

JAMES 1:9-12

HANDICAPPED THINKING—$250 FINE

"Believers who are poor have something to BOAST about, for God has honored them. And those who are rich should boast that God has humbled them. They will fade away like a little flower in the field. The hot sun rises and the grass withers; the little flower droops and falls, and its beauty fades away. In the same way, the rich will fade away with all of their achievements. God blesses those who patiently endure testing and temptation. Afterward they will receive the crown of life that God has promised to those who love him."(NLT)

DEFINITION: Perspective

1. a view or vista, mental view or outlook

DISCUSSION

Parking in a handicap spot can cost you up to $250 if you are not handicapped. Parking in "handicapped" thinking can cost you, too! God loves to take this way of thinking and change it to a Godly **perspective**—without the fine! James is teaching us that both the poor and the rich have trials. Both have reason to boast before God, both will be equally blessed when they wait patiently during tough times, and both will receive the crown of life that God has promised. There is eternal life for **all** who believe in Jesus. Yet, do you ever get handicapped in your thinking that the more you HAVE, the less trials you will experience?

Jesse did NOT want to go back to school after Christmas break. She knew her best friend, Alena, would be wearing the newest and latest fashion. Jesse's family didn't have the money like her friend. But Jesse and Alena had been friends since 1st grade, and they even believed in Jesus the same night on the youth retreat. Still, Jesse thought that Alena had it MUCH easier because she had "more." Returning to school, Jesse noticed Alena's new clothes but also noticed that Alena wasn't being herself.

"What's wrong?," Jesse asked. Alena sighed, "Jesse, my parents told me they are getting divorced. I am so sad. I'm so glad to have a friend like you. You never seem to have problems." Jesse was shocked. Maybe her way of thinking was all wrong. Maybe just because you had more material "things" didn't mean that you had less problems. One thing she DID know. God was her strength, and He would help BOTH of them. "Alena, we have a lot to learn. Together, with God, we'll get through this and . . . by the way, I love your new jeans!"

DIRECTIONAL QUESTIONS

1. Reading James 1:9-12, what do these verses mean to you?

2. In what ways do the poor and rich have to boast? Why do you think James puts emphasis on the "rich fading away with all their achievements?"

3. Earthly riches do NOT mark a person's TRUE wealth. Read 1 Timothy 6: 7-12. What does it mean to be spiritually rich?

4. Who will be blessed by enduring trials? What is their reward?

"YOU CAN'T TAKE A U-HAUL TO HEAVEN."

BACKROAD DRIVIN'

UNDER the pressure of trials, we ALL have to learn how to LEAN on God, whether rich or poor, big or small. God does not have favorites. In fact, He loves ALL His children equally. This is a U-Turn many of us need to take. As servants of God, we are to BOAST about ALL that He is and ALL He has done for us—not what we do or do not have. Death is a quick reminder that we cannot take anything with us when we leave this earth. It also reminds us that when we BELIEVE in Jesus, we will receive the crown of glory and live FOREVER with Him. That is Godly PERSPECTIVE and not handicapped thinking!

ADDITIONAL SIGHTSEEING

Look up John 3:16, 1 John 1:9, Romans 8:17, and Ephesians 1:11-14

We are spiritually RICH in Jesus. Identify the four reasons from these verses. (Answers on bottom)

John 3:16

1 John 1:9

Romans 8:17

Ephesians 1:11-14

In Jesus, we: 1. have eternal life. 2. are forgiven of our sins. 3. are heirs of God and share in His glory. 4. are chosen and marked by the Holy Spirit.

STOP and write down your prayers.

Lord,

Thank You that You do not have favorites and that You offer the crown of eternal life to EVERYONE who believes in Christ. I pray to be spiritually rich in You—to know and depend on You more and not the material things of this world. Help my handicapped way of thinking and change it into a Godly perspective.

Amen.

James 1:9-12

JAMES 1:13-15
APPLY THE BRAKES!

"And REMEMBER, when you are being **tempted**, do not say, "God is tempting me." God is never tempted to do wrong, and He never tempts anyone else. Temptation comes from our OWN desires, which entice us and drag us away. These desires give birth to sinful actions. And when sin is allowed to grow, it gives birth to death." (NLT)

DEFINITION: Temptation

1. a desire to do something, especially something wrong or unwise

DISCUSSION

Put on the BRAKES! What does James tell us about temptation? It is born out of our natural desires that drag us away from what we KNOW is right. God has given us HIS directional road signs for a reason. He loves us and KNOWS the best path we should take. But the world also gives us road signs that ultimately lead down the **wrong** highway. Before we know it, we are lost with no detours in sight.

Evelyn and Adam were studying at the library for History when Evelyn got a great idea to cross the street to grab a burger at the Apple Core Cafe. Even though their parents told them to stay at the library, she convinced her friend. "Come on Adam, no one will know! Besides, I've heard their cheeseburgers are the BEST in town! Just look at the sign. You can almost taste them!" Evelyn said. Adam hadn't eaten much that day, and he agreed that it did look a LOT better than the fruit his Mom had packed. "OK, let's go. We have to go fast though, I only have 30 minutes before my Mom gets here," Adam replied. While they were eating, Adam saw his Mom pull up to the Library. "Oh no! I am totally in trouble. My Mom is here 10 minutes early. Now what am I supposed to do? It's all your fault, Evelyn. Thanks a lot!" Adam said as he wiped the ketchup off his face, grabbed his backpack, and headed across the street.

Does this story sound familiar? It might if you have read Genesis 3:1-13. Satan enticed Adam and Eve to fall into sin and disobey God from the beginning of time. He is still at it today—enticing us to disobey God and fall into temptation. But, we have a CHOICE. Let's choose to put on the BRAKES to evil desires and not blame others for our own actions. Choosing to **Follow God's Road Signs** will ALWAYS get you where you should go, without the headaches and detours!

DIRECTIONAL QUESTIONS

1. What are the most common temptations you and your friends face today?

2. What temptations are you struggling with this week? How can you "APPLY THE BRAKES" when tempted and put your TRUST in God?

3. Do you often blame others for your actions (like in the story)?

4. Reading James 1:13-15, what are the three stages of temptation? Where does it start, how does it grow, and where does it lead?

"I Brake for God"
- Bumper Sticker

BACKROAD DRIVIN'

Just like villains in today's movies, we also have a villain in our world. The difference is, he is NOT an actor. His name is Satan, and he is real. In John 12:31, he is called "the ruler of this world" and the reason behind MANY of our temptations. His sole purpose is to get us as FAR away from believing in God as possible. If he can achieve this, then we are following his road signs and not God's perfect plan. We need to be reminded that **GOD is in control of ALL things**, even the agenda of the villain (Job 1:12). For reasons we may never understand, God allowed Satan in the Garden of Eden, and He allows him to deceive us still today. As believers in Jesus, Do NOT choose to be tempted by evil. **Put on the BRAKES** and drive the RIGHT way toward God.

ADDITIONAL SIGHTSEEING

Look up 1 Peter 5:8-9, Luke 4:1-13, and Matthew 6:13

With God's help, you can fight your desires before you fall into temptation. Identify your temptation and three ways to fight against it from these verses.

1 Peter 5:8-9

Luke 4:1-13

Matthew 6:13

We can overcome temptation by: 1. having self-control, being alert, and standing firm in our faith. 2. the Word of God. 3. prayer.

24

and write down your prayers.

Lord,

Please remind me to PUT ON the BRAKES when I am tempted to do something wrong or unwise. Help me to be strong in my faith and always set an example for You. When I feel the urge to sin, I pray to STOP and turn the other direction, not allowing temptation to grow. You will lead me in the way I should go!

Amen.

James 1:13-15

JAMES 1:16-18

RED LIGHT, GREEN LIGHT

"Don't be deceived, my dear brothers. Every good and perfect **gift** is from above, coming down from the Father of the heavenly lights, who does not change like shifting shadows. He chose to give us birth through the word of truth, that we might be a kind of first fruits of all he created."

DEFINITION: Gift

1. something given; a present
2. special ability, talent

DISCUSSION

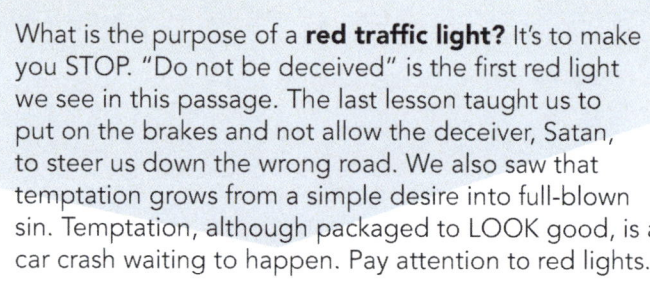

What is the purpose of a **red traffic light?** It's to make you STOP. "Do not be deceived" is the first red light we see in this passage. The last lesson taught us to put on the brakes and not allow the deceiver, Satan, to steer us down the wrong road. We also saw that temptation grows from a simple desire into full-blown sin. Temptation, although packaged to LOOK good, is a car crash waiting to happen. Pay attention to red lights.

The purpose of a **green light** is to move you ahead. That's what God is telling you to do. Don't get stuck concentrating on the trials and temptations you might be going through. Persevere and look to the truth. SEE that every good thing you have, every talent you have been given, every gift, and every meal that sustains you, is from GOD! God is the PERFECT gift giver!

The purpose of a **yellow light** is to slow you down. When you STOP being deceived and take time and GO to God's Word, you will be FILLED with strength and FAITH. Think of it like filling your car up with gas. You are filling up your heart with God's Word.

In Genesis 1:27, the Bible says that you are created in GOD's image. God chose you, over every creature He created, to give YOU life through the Word of truth. The Word is the Bible, and it is the ONLY map you will ever need. All goodness is from God, all gifts are from God, and all truth is from God. **Let's start following His lights.** After all, God is the "Father of all lights," —the STOPS, the GO's, and the SLOW DOWN's.

DIRECTIONAL QUESTIONS

1. What are the good and perfect gifts God has given you?

2. Deceptive means *tending to deceive or having power to mislead.* How are temptations deceiving, misleading, and packaged to look good? What do you think about this quote?

> "Many of our troubles occur because we base our choices on unreliable authorities: culture 'everyone is doing it,' reason 'it seemed logical,' or emotion 'it just felt right.'" ~ Rick Warren

3. How can you stop, go, and slow down when you are facing trials and temptations?

4. What are the truths about God in this passage? (I found six.)

**"YOUR WORD IS TRUTH."
JOHN 17:17**

BACKROAD DRIVIN'

GENESIS 2:7 says that God formed Adam and breathed into him the breath of LIFE and he became a living being. The same is true of you. The GOD of the universe breathed His VERY BREATH into YOU! And this was just the beginning. God not only gave you life, but also gifts, talents, kindness, joy, love, and wisdom. He gave you the Bible (which is the Word of truth), eternity, Jesus, and it is ALL GOOD! Pardon my slang, but IF IT AIN'T GOOD, IT AIN'T GOD! This is a simple truth that works. What is deceiving you today that you "think" is good, but is not? Base your choices on the goodness of God alone. STOP being deceived. GO to the One who made you, and SLOW down to unwrap His gifts.

ADDITIONAL SIGHTSEEING

Look up John 3:16, Romans 6:23, Romans 12:6-8, and 2 Timothy 1:7

What are GIFTS God has given to you? Identify your gifts from these verses and give thanks for God is the giver of every good gift!

John 3:16

Romans 6:23

Romans 12:6-8

2 Timothy 1:7

God has given us the gift of: 1. believing in Jesus. 2. eternal life. 3. service, teaching, encouraging, ... 4. power, love, and self-discipline.

STOP
and write down your prayers.

Lord,

Help me STOP when I am being deceived, especially when temptation looks good. I pray to always GO to Your truth and SLOW down to study Your Word. Help me to concentrate on the gifts You have given me and not the trials I am going through.

Amen.

James 1:16-18

JAMES 1:19-21
BUCKLE UP—IT WILL SAVE YOUR LIFE

"My dear brothers, take note of this: Everyone should be quick to **listen**, slow to speak and slow to become angry, for man's anger does not bring about the righteous life that God desires. Therefore, get rid of all moral filth and the evil that is so prevalent and humbly accept the word planted in you, which can save you."

DEFINITION: Listen

1. to give attention with the ear; attend closely for the purpose of hearing
2. to pay attention

DISCUSSION

Do you think there is a reason why God gave us TWO ears and ONE mouth? Maybe He designed us to be better **listeners** than speakers! James is telling us that we need to take note and pay attention. Everyone should be QUICK to listen but SLOW to speak and SLOW to anger. Remember, these verses are still in the context of "counting it all JOY" in the middle of hard circumstances. Now, God is giving us driving instructions on just how to do that, and not this . . .

"I've had it! I'm so mad, I could scream. I am tired of everyone always coming into my room and taking whatever they want. I'm tired of school and too much homework. I'm tired of ballet, piano, and my parents expecting way too much. And, I'm tired of you, yes you. So please, get OUT of my room!" Emily slammed the door on her brother, sat down, and cried. She thought getting angry and yelling would make her feel better, but it just made her feel worse.

We think our anger is acceptable when we are having a hard day. But the truth is, our anger isn't pleasing to God at all. Anger is the vehicle to many pains in life and often, we are responsible. It's like going

through life without a seat belt. Having a quick temper is similar to getting into a wreck without the safety of being buckled in. When we crash, our anger not only hurts us but also others. God's instructions to be slow to anger keeps us from crashing and protects those around us. Listening, instead of talking and getting angry, is the first protective measure. The second instruction on the safety list is getting rid of all the filth and evil in our lives—all the stuff that pollutes our relationship with God. When you feel an accident about to happen, RUN to God's Word. It will save your life.

DIRECTIONAL QUESTIONS

1. Why do you think God gave us two ears and one mouth?

2. How is a quick temper like going through life without a seat belt?

3. What filth and evil do you need to get rid of? Sometimes evil in our lives can be obvious and sometimes less obvious. What are examples of subtle ways evil can block your relationship with God?

4. What do you think it means to "humbly accept the word planted in you which can save you?" How can God's Word save you?

"BUCKLE UP. IT'S THE LAW"

BACKROAD DRIVIN'

The Word of God is described as a seed planted in one's heart. Just like any seed, it needs water to grow. Accepting God's Word, spending time in Scripture, praying, and having relationships with other girls that believe in Jesus is the **water** that nourishes the Word of God in us. What happens to a plant when it doesn't have water? It dies. What happens to us when we stop nourishing the Word of God planted in our hearts? We stop growing. God tells us to get rid of the filth and evil that prohibits the Word of God from growing in us. This is another safety measure. Having God's Word alive and growing in our hearts can save us from many crashes in life.

ADDITIONAL SIGHTSEEING

Look up 2 Timothy 4:17-18, 2 Thessalonians 3:3, 1 Corinthians 10:13, and Psalm 91:3-7

God saves us from many troubles in life. Just like wearing a seat belt, He can protect us from getting hurt. Find other ways that God is our protector. (Answers on bottom)

2 Timothy 4:17-18

_____

_____

2 Thessalonians 3:3

_____

_____

1 Corinthians 10:13

_____

_____

Psalm 91:3-7

_____

_____

The Lord protects us: 1. and gives us strength. 2. from evil. 3. while we are being tempted. 4. from danger.

and write down your prayers.

Lord,

YOU are my protection. I pray to be QUICK to listen, slow to speak, and slow to anger. When I feel my temper getting hot, I pray to allow Your Word to grow inside me. Get rid of the filth in me that blocks my relationship with You. Teach me to buckle up in Your Word, which can save me from many crashes in this life!

Amen.

James 1:19-21

JAMES 1:22-25

GOD'S GPS

"Do not merely listen to the word, and so deceive yourselves. **Do** what it says. Anyone who listens to the word but does not do what it says is like a man who looks at his face in a mirror and, after looking at himself, goes away and immediately forgets what he looks like. But the man who looks intently into the perfect law that gives freedom, and continues to do this, not forgetting what he has heard, but doing it—he will be blessed in what he does."

DEFINITION: Do

1. to bring to pass, to carry out 2. perform, execute
3. commit, bring about, to give freely, to put forth

DISCUSSION

Have you ever gotten a new phone or a game and did not read the instructions? What about studying for a test? Have you ever glanced over the notes only to find out that during the test you had forgotten everything? The Bible is our instruction book for life, or better yet, our GPS. Only it doesn't stand for "global positioning system" but rather **God's Positioning System.** The Bible, like any GPS or instruction manual, is meant to be read, remembered, and acted upon ... not forgotten. Why? Because no matter what trial we are going through, God is ALWAYS there to help us when we get lost. But we must do our part! Tracking your location isn't enough. You have to listen to the instructions and **do** what it says.

Anne Marie got home late after basketball practice and was exhausted. She could barely keep her eyes open as she studied for her history test the next day. "I've studied enough," she thought. "I'll give it one more look tomorrow before the exam." The next day, Anne Marie was kicking herself for not studying harder. During the test, she couldn't remember the three branches of government or the capitols of all the states. She thought a quick glance that morning would work, but she was mistaken. Anne Marie had forgotten everything.

In the last lesson, we looked at being quick to listen. In this lesson, we learn that listening alone won't deepen our faith and give us the wisdom we need during trials. We need to **act** on God's Word, **study** it with intention, and **do** what it says. Applying Biblical instruction to our everyday lives will help us persevere (James 1:3) during the pot holes of life as well as BLESS us along the way. Depending on the Word of God matures our faith and gives us direction. Trusting in God's GPS, the Bible, is ALL we need to make straight A's!

DIRECTIONAL QUESTIONS

1. Have you ever thrown away an instruction manual? Why? Did you look for it when something went wrong?

2. How can simply listening to God's Word and not acting on it be deceiving? Why do we need to be listeners AND doers of God's Word?

3. What do you think the word *intently* means, and why would this make a difference in how we study God's Word? What are the results?

4. What is the "perfect law that gives us freedom?" How does God's Word give us freedom? How will doing it BLESS us in all we do?

"JUST DO IT"

BACKROAD DRIVIN'

To look intently into God's Word is to carefully and continually STUDY it. It is not a one-time test that you take just to get a good grade and then forget all the information. Imagine what would happen if drivers took the driver's exam and then forgot all the rules of the road. People would be running red lights, speeding through stop signs, and crashing into each other! The Bible is to be purposefully read and re-read, especially in times of trial and temptation. James 1:25 reminds us that when we act on what we have heard and continue to study God's Word, it will not only save us (James 1:21), and give us freedom (James 1:25), but will also **bless us in what we do.** The Word of God gives us wisdom, direction, freedom, blessing, and guidance . . . the perfect GPS!

ADDITIONAL SIGHTSEEING

Look up Luke 24:12, John 20:5, and John 20:11

The word "intently" occurs five times in the New Testament. It means to *stoop down in order to look in.* What were Peter and Mary **intently** looking for? What did they see and was it what they expected? Why should we intently study God's Word? (Sometimes what we see is not what we expect!)

Luke 24:12

John 20:5

John 20:11

Peter INTENTLY studied the empty tomb. Mary bent over to LOOK in the tomb.

STOP and write down your prayers.

Lord,

I pray to study Your Word with passion and purpose. I do not want to forget the perfect law that frees me from the stresses and misdirections of this world. I pray not to get lost, but to trust in Your GPS, especially during the trials and temptations.

Amen.

James 1:22-25

JAMES 1:26-27

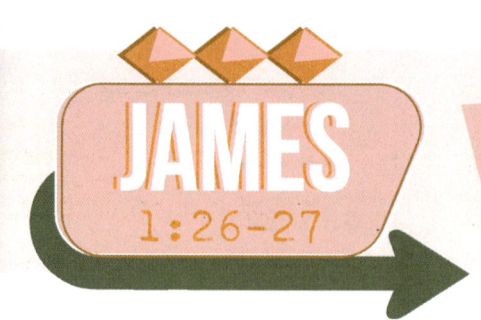

WALK THE TALK

"If anyone considers himself religious and yet does not keep a tight rein on his tongue, he deceives himself and his religion is worthless. Religion that God our Father accepts as pure and faultless is this: to look after orphans and widows in their distress and to keep oneself from being **polluted** by the world."

DEFINITION: Polluted

1. made unclean or impure; contaminated
2. morally harmful; corrupt

DISCUSSION

We made it! Today we are studying the final verses in James, chapter one. Notice that three times in the first chapter, James mentions the word deceived. Here we find that we are deceived if we consider ourselves religious but can't control our tongue. What does it mean to be religious? Is it going to church? Being in Bible study? Youth Group? Confirmation? Putting your allowance in the offering plate? Being religious can mean a lot of things, but in the first part of this particular passage, James points out what it is NOT.

Gretchen was super excited that Kayla Jenkins was riding home on the bus. Gretchen had always looked up to Kayla from afar. Kayla was pretty, smart, stylish, president of the Service Club, and even went to her youth group. But by the end of the ride, Gretchen wasn't so sure Kayla was religious at all. During the entire ride, she said horrible things about one of Gretchen's best friends. She made fun of her clothes and even talked about her single mother being unable to afford a field trip to the aquarium. Gretchen's heart was broken. People just aren't what they seem.

Many people appear to be "religious," but their hearts are far from knowing and trusting in God. Attending church, youth group, or even Bible study is very important, but God knows when these actions are just for show—especially when we are careless with our words. We are certainly not deceiving God; we are only deceiving ourselves. We need to WALK THE TALK! Religion that God accepts as pure is looking after orphans, widows, and NOT being polluted by the world. Walking the talk is about taking God seriously and obeying His words. In the last lesson we talked about not only listening to His words, but also DOING what they say. Let's choose NOT to be contaminated by the ways of this world, but instead choose to ONLY **follow HIS road signs.**

DIRECTIONAL QUESTIONS

1. What does being religious mean to you? Is there a difference between being "religious" and being a Christian?

2. What does it mean to keep a tight rein on your tongue? How can having an explosive tongue be deceiving and harmful to Christianity?

3. What are ways you can look after orphans and widows?

4. How are you or your friends being polluted by the world? What are ways to avoid this situation?

"CHRISTIANITY BEGINS WHERE RELIGION ENDS." –ANONYMOUS

BACKROAD DRIVIN'

Keeping a tight rein on your tongue is a consistent theme in the book of James. God must know how bad it hurts when you hear or say something ugly about someone else. Look at these verses:

Proverbs 34:13 "Keep your tongue from evil and your lips from speaking lies, turn from evil and do good; seek peace and pursue it."

Proverbs 10:19 "When words are many, sin is not absent, but he that holds his tongue is wise."

Proverbs 12:18 "Reckless words pierce like a sword, but the tongue of the wise brings healing."

Our words are powerful, and you can either speak evil or blessing. Let's choose to represent GOD this week with our words and actions! Speak with truth and wisdom, do good, and WALK THE TALK.

ADDITIONAL SIGHTSEEING

Look up: James 1:16,17, James 1:22, and James 1:26

The word deceived occurs three times in first chapter of James. What are the specific issues in which we are being deceived? (Answers on bottom)

James 1:16,17

James 1:22

James 1:26

The LIES are 1. God is the deceiver. 2. We can just listen to the Word and not do what it says. 3. We can go through the motions of being a Christian and not control our tongue.

STOP and write down your prayers.

Lord,

Help me to take You more seriously. I pray You would help me to hold my tongue and that I would not be polluted by the ways of this world. I know when I speak with reckless words it not only hurts others but YOU. Teach me to how to care for the orphans and widows and to always be a good example for YOU!

Amen.

James 1:26-27

JAMES 1:1-27

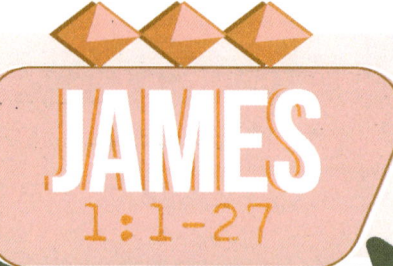

Artist Workshop Ahead

JOY JAR

HOW TO:

"Consider it pure JOY, my brothers and sisters, whenever you face trials of many kinds..."

THE JOY jar

INSTRUCTIONS:

1. Select and clean a container.

2. (Optional) If you are using a tin container, you can punch two holes in the side of your can using a hammer and a nail. Simply hammer two small holes in opposite sides of the container an inch from the top. These holes will be used for handles.

3. Measure and glue fabric (cut to size) onto the container.

4. If you choose to make a handle, attach your handles using 15 inches of floral wire.

5. Using a low-temp glue gun or Elmer's glue, embellish your container with fabric, ribbon, trim, buttons, and more.

6. Print out the JOY JAR Scripture onto cardstock paper, cut, and attach with wire. Remember, this is YOUR JOY JAR ~ Consider is JOY!

ART STOP

42

ART SUPPLIES:

- Container (aluminum can or glass jar: peanut butter jar, yogurt container, soup, or tomato can)
- Glue
- Low-Temp Hot Glue Gun and Glue Sticks
- Foam Brush
- Fabric
- Ribbon, Wire, Yarn, Cording, Trim, etc.
- Floral Wire for handles (8-12 guage)
- Scissors
- Embellishments (buttons, sequins, etc.)
- Hammer and Nail
- Printer and Cardstock Paper

Tip: Wire in the art demonstration is from the Dollar Tree

DOWNLOAD THE JOY JAR ART VIDEO and TEMPLATE @ **thouartexalted.com/James-art**

The password is: **GREEN LIGHT**

Chapter One Overview: Consider it JOY when you go through many trials because perseverance builds maturity. Every GOOD and PERFECT gift is from above. Be quick to listen, slow to speak, and slow to become angry. Do not merely listen to the Word, DO what it SAYS. Keep yourself from being polluted by this world.

JOY JAR: Fill your jar with the trials you experience. Write them down on pieces of paper, fold them up, and put them in your JOY JAR. A week, a month, or even a year later, take out a piece of paper and open it up. See how GOD has used that trial in your life to make your faith stronger and better. Remember to consider it JOY. GOD is doing an amazing work through you!

JAMES 2:1-4

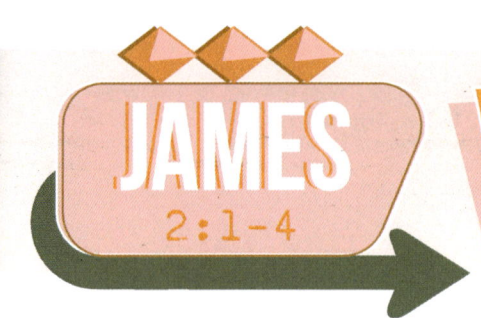

STOP THE POLLUTION

"My brothers as believers in our glorious Lord Jesus Christ, don't show **favoritism**. Suppose a man comes into your meeting wearing a gold ring and fine clothes, and a poor man in shabby clothes also comes in. If you show special attention to the man wearing fine clothes and say, 'Here's a good seat for you,' but say to the poor man, 'You stand there' or 'Sit on the floor by my feet,' have you not discriminated among yourselves and become judges with evil thoughts?'"

DEFINITION: Favoritism

1. the practice of giving unfair preferential treatment to one person or group at the expense of another.

DISCUSSION

I am sure there are MANY things you favor over another. For example, you might favor bananas over brussel spouts or history over science. But the issue is not favoring a fruit over a vegetable or which subject you like the best. The real issue is favoring one person over the other, and we must admit that we are **ALL guilty** of this charge. The believers that James was addressing centuries ago were guilty, too!

Piper walked into the room and everyone stared with fixed attention. She was always a good singer but now that she had made it to the top three on AMERICAN IDOL, she was amazing! She looked beautiful, and Hollywood had definitely made its mark. Her makeup was spotless, her earrings matched the gold circles in her dress, and her voice was angelic. Piper had reached stardom, and I wanted her to see me! As I was jumping up to catch Piper's attention, Caroline tried to stand next to me. "Oh, not now," I thought. "I am NOT in the mood to hear one of your dramatic saga stories." I brushed Caroline off and made my way to the front of the stage. Piper was MUCH more important.

Just because someone is rich, famous, or even popular, doesn't mean we should give that person special attention. God knows how easy it is to give someone higher recognition just because of WHO they are. That's why James is telling us very simply, DO NOT SHOW FAVORITISM. When we do, we are judging that person by their outward circumstance over their inward character. This is NOT **Following God's Road Signs,** but rather the ways of this world. The previous verse (James 1:27) reminds us that pure religion is looking after the poor, the widows, and not being polluted by the things of this world. Favoritism and judgment ARE the pollution that we need to toss out.

DIRECTIONAL QUESTIONS

1. As a believer in Jesus, why do you think it is important NOT to show favoritism? (Remember James in introduction)

2. Can you think of examples when you have showed favoritism? Have you ever been judged? How did you feel?

3. How are we discriminating and "judging with evil thoughts" when we show favoritism?

4. How is favoritism and judgment like pollution? What toxic gases are we emitting?

"DON'T PICK ON PEOPLE, JUMP ON THEIR FAILURES, CRITICIZE THEIR FAULTS - UNLESS, OF COURSE, YOU WANT THE SAME TREATMENT." MATT. 7:1 (MSG)

BACKROAD DRIVIN'

Just like you must service a car to prevent toxic gas emissions, you need to service your heart to avoid spewing toxic behavior. Gossip, favoritism, and judgment are a few of these dangerous fumes. We learn in Romans 2:11 that God does not show favoritism. WHY? Because He created ALL of us in His image. Just as there are many makes of cars: sports cars, SUV's, mini vans, sedans, etc., there are many models of the human race: Caucasion, African-American, European, Asian, male, female, etc. But we ALL have one thing in common—we are made in GOD's likeness! As believers, we need to look under the hoods of our hearts often and diagnose any pollution. When our hearts get clogged with polluted elements, such as favoritism, **we are due for maintenance**. Let's check our hearts often and keep the roads safe!

ADDITIONAL SIGHTSEEING

Look up Galatians 5:22-23, Ephesians 5:29, Ephesians 5:32, and Philippians 2:3

What can FILL your heart to help you AVOID the toxic gases of favoritism and judgment? (Answers on bottom)

Galatians 5:22-23

Ephesians 5:29

Ephesians 5:32

Philippians 2:3

We can fill our hearts with 1. the FRUITS of the Spirit. 2. words that build one another up and encourage. 3. being kind, compassionate, and forgiving. 4. considering others better than yourselves.

STOP
and write down your prayers.

Lord,

Help me to perform daily maintenance on my heart to make sure I am not emitting any toxic gases. I know that gossip, showing favoritism, and judging others are hurtful and mean. I want my heart to glorify YOU and only YOU.

Amen.

James 2:1-4

JAMES 2:5-9

LIFETIME WARRANTY, GUARANTEED!

"Listen to me, dear brothers and sisters. Hasn't God chosen the poor in this world to be rich in faith? Aren't they the ones who will **inherit** the Kingdom he promised to those who love him? But you dishonor the poor! Isn't it the rich who oppress you and drag you into court? Aren't they the ones who slander Jesus Christ, whose noble name you bear?" (NLT)

"If you really keep the royal law found in Scripture, 'Love your neighbor as yourself,' you are doing right."

DEFINITION: Inherit

1. to come into possession of or receive, especially as a right or divine portion

DISCUSSION

At this point in our journey together, we should be quite aware that **Following God's Road Signs** is VERY different from following the signs of this world. The world says to have a pity party when life doesn't go your way. **God says to be joyful.** The world says God is the one who tempts you to do bad things. **God says it is your own sinful nature.** The world says it's enough just to listen to God's Word. **God says do what it says.** The world says take notice of the rich and famous. **God says look after the poor.**

Laura met Grace in the trade markets of Arusha, Tanzania. Laura had been volunteering in Africa and was picking up some last-minute, small souvenirs when some colorful painted birds caught her eye. As she approached booth 91, it was Grace's warm smile and loving eyes that drew Laura into her booth, but more so, into her heart. Being a million miles away from her home in Tennessee, Laura began to sense more than a simple purchase, but an everlasting friendship. Laura returned to Grace's booth two days later with a desire to know more about this woman. Grace graciously showed Laura her home, her children, her loom, and her heart. Five years later, Laura and Grace remain close friends.

"Grace gave to me in a way that I had never experienced before. She didn't have much to hang her hat on, but she had a wealth of hospitality and was rich in the kind of faith many of us only read about. Here I was, a young, bright-eyed, college student thinking I was going to make my way to Africa and make an impact on someone, and I left there feeling overwhelmed with the impact that Africa had on me."
- Laura Bolton Rowe

DIRECTIONAL QUESTIONS

1. What does it mean to receive an inheritance?

2. Who will inherit the Kingdom of God? (verse 5)

3. Laura teaches us to "love our neighbor as ourselves." How did Laura go beyond the lines of culture, race, and perhaps her own comfort by reaching out to Grace?

4. The poor in this world are rich in faith. How was Grace rich even when she had "nothing to hang her hat on?"

"IF YOU JUDGE PEOPLE, YOU HAVE NO TIME TO LOVE THEM."
-MOTHER TERESA

BACKROAD DRIVIN'

All who love God and believe in His son, Jesus Christ will receive the **inherit**ance of His Kingdom, whether rich or poor. Receiving the inheritance is not a matter of material wealth, but about the condition of the heart. Jesus, the perfect Son of God, died because our sinful nature separates us from the Father. When we believe in Jesus, our sin is forgiven and once again, we are joined in perfect relationship with God, GUARANTEED. Our belief makes us children of God and daughters of the King! We receive an inheritance of the Kingdom that is overflowing with riches both in this life and forever. In the movie *Cars*, Lightning McQueen's sponsor was RUSTEEZE, a cure for rust. In the motion picture of life, our sponsor is JESUS, a cure for sin. Let's share the **good news** like Laura. We are indeed RICH in faith when we believe in the King of Kings!

ADDITIONAL SIGHTSEEING

Look up Titus 3:3-7, John 1:12, 1 John 1:7, and I Peter 2:9

What inheritance of the KINGDOM do we receive when we believe in Jesus? (Answers on bottom)

Titus 3:3-7

John 1:12

1 John 1:7

I Peter 2:9

When we believe in Jesus, we receive the 1. Holy Spirit and eternal life. 2. right to become children of God. 3. purification of sin. 4. blessing of being God's very own.

STOP
and write down your prayers.

Lord,

I am indeed RICH in faith when I believe in You! Help me to reach out to those who need Your love today. Thank You that I am a daughter of the **KING** and for the inheritance I have of abundant and **ETERNA**L life with You—guaranteed!

Amen.

James 2:5-9

JAMES 2:9-13

NO TRAFFIC VIOLATION!

"If you really keep the royal law found in Scripture, "Love your neighbor as yourself," you are doing right. But if you show favoritism, you sin and are convicted by the law as lawbreakers. For whoever keeps the whole law and yet stumbles at just one point is guilty of breaking it all. For he who said, 'Do not commit adultery,' also said, 'Do not commit murder.' If you do not commit adultery but do commit murder, you have become a lawbreaker. Speak and act as those who are going to be judged by the law that gives freedom, because judgment without mercy will be shown to anyone who has been **merciful**. Mercy triumphs over judgment!"

DEFINITION: Merciful

1. showing or exercising mercy, compassion or forgiveness shown toward someone whom it is within one's power to punish or harm
2. bringing someone relief from something unpleasant

DISCUSSION

At first glance, these passages might seem really confusing! It all boils down to **loving others**, **loving God**, and **showing mercy**. We saw the verse "love your neighbor as yourself" demonstrated in last lesson's story of Laura and Grace. It's important to repeat this verse again because when we are sincerely loving others, without showing judgment or favoritism, we are doing what God says AND showing His mercy.

The policeman had every right to give me a speeding ticket. After all, I was speeding. My car was taking me to tutor for an after-school program, but my mind was taking me back to what happened to Annie that day at school. Why did kids have to be so mean? Especially with ones who "claim" to be Christians. Annie was a sweet girl, maybe a little awkward, but nonetheless, very kind. She was new at school and was trying out for cheerleading. At tryouts, she forgot her routine and tripped over her own shoe string. Embarrassing? Yes. Did it help her make the team? No. Annie slowly got up yet quickly left in tears. While I was driving, the thought hit me. No one helped her. No one showed compassion. Not the coaches, not the girls, not even me. I felt ashamed. Who do I claim to be?

Here I was, heading to help kids with math, feeling so good about myself. Yeah, right. I couldn't even help a friend who was mortified in front of the whole gym. As I could hear the footsteps of the policeman, I prayed silently that God would forgive my judgmental heart. I prayed also for Annie, that she would forgive me for not helping her. As I pulled out my driver's license, the police officer got an emergency call and had to leave immediately. "Looks like God had mercy on you today," he chuckled. With a deep sigh of relief, I said, "Yeah, you have no idea. You have no idea."

DIRECTIONAL QUESTIONS

1. In the past week, how have you "loved your neighbor as yourself?"

2. Why do you think we are guilty of breaking the "whole law" when we just break one part of it? (James 2:10)

3. Some people see God's law as restrictive and boring. James 2:12 describes God's law, or God's Word, as giving freedom? How is this?

4. Rewrite the story of Annie and add a BIG dose of mercy. How could the story change? How has Jesus shown you mercy and not judgment? (See definition)

> "I CHOOSE KINDNESS... I WILL BE KIND TO THE POOR, FOR THEY ARE ALONE. KIND TO THE RICH, FOR THEY ARE AFRAID. AND KIND TO THE UNKIND, FOR SUCH IS HOW GOD HAS TREATED ME." -MAX LUCADO

BACKROAD DRIVIN'

Matthew 5:7 says, "Blessed are the merciful, for they will be shown mercy." Jesus continually teaches that we are to show the same love for others that He has shown for us. Romans 5:8 talks about this amazing MERCIFUL LOVE that God has for his children.

> "God demonstrates His own LOVE in this: While we were still sinners, Christ died for us."

Even though Jesus had done NOTHING wrong, He knew the ONLY way we could have a perfect relationship with His Father was that HE take on our sin. When we believe in Jesus, he takes our sin, and in exchange, we get to take on His perfect nature. THAT IS MERCY. When we fully acknowledge what Christ has done for us, our hearts should be exploding with **mercy**! Judgment and favoritism are the road signs of this world. Let's take the 911 call instead and have a servant's heart to **love others.**

ADDITIONAL SIGHTSEEING

Look up 1 Timothy 15-16, Ephesians 2:4-6, and Micah 6:8

Without a doubt, God is merciful. But He also wants us to BE merciful. What do these passages tell us about mercy? (Answers on bottom)

1 Timothy 15-16

Ephesians 2:4-6

Micah 6:8

Answers: 1. Jesus showed us mercy to display His unlimited patience and offer eternal salvation. 2. We are made alive in Christ because of God's mercy. 3. God wants us to love mercy and walk humbly with Him.

STOP
and write down your prayers.

Lord,

Thank You for Your compassion and forgiveness. Help me to show the same mercy to others around me. I have so much to be thankful for. Sometimes it's easy to show favoritism. Help me to ALWAYS have a servant's heart.

Amen.

James 2:9-13

JAMES 2:14-18

A PORSCHE WITH NO POWER

"What good is it, my brothers, if a man claims to have **faith** but has no deeds? Can such faith save him? Suppose a brother or sister is without clothes and daily food. If one of you says to him, 'Go, I wish you well; keep warm and well fed,' but does nothing about his physical needs, what good is it? In the same way, faith by itself, if it is not accompanied by action, is dead. But someone will say, 'You have faith; I have deeds. 'Show me your faith without deeds, and I will show you my faith by what I DO.'"

DEFINITION: Faith

1. The conviction that God exists and is the creator and ruler of all things, the provider and bestower of eternal salvation through Christ*

    a. The religious beliefs of Christians

*Definition from *Blue Letter Bible*

DISCUSSION

Can you imagine a Porsche with no power or a Maserati without a motor? This is what faith without works looks like. Remember studying James 1:22? If we only listen to God's Word and do not DO what it says, we are only deceiving ourselves. God wants us to take our faith and put it into ACTION. Without action, **faith is dead.**

"I promise, I'll be there. I know I have worked late this week, but I WILL be at your game tonight," Lauren's Dad said. Everything in her wanted to believe him, but she knew that if he didn't show up, it would just be another broken promise.

"I will be praying for you," Lilly yelled from the car door. But the busy day got away from her and she never even thought again about her prayer for her sister's dentist appointment."

"You bet! I would love to help serve at the soup kitchen Friday night," Kaiden replied as she spoke to her friend. But Friday came and went. Kaiden had completely forgotten about her intention to help serve with her friend.

While good intentions and promises are good, without action, they fall short. Similarly, our faith falls short when we don't put it into action. James is telling us that TRUE faith has "feet" on it. When we honestly BELIEVE in our Christian convictions, it's only natural that we act upon our FAITH. The Message Bible says that faith and works, works and faith, fit together hand in glove (vs.18). Remember that when we look intently into the perfect law that gives FREEDOM and DO what it says, we will be BLESSED (James 1: 25). Let's put some power behind our faith and take our actions on the highway.

DIRECTIONAL QUESTIONS

1. What good it is to own a Maserati that just sits in the garage? What good is it if a man claims to have faith but has no deeds or works? Can you make a comparison?

2. Why do you think it is important to have faith AND deeds? Can one survive without the other?

3. As believers in Christ, how do your actions reflect your faith?

4. Can you identify with any of the stories about faith without action? How would these stories be different using faith and deeds together?

> "... GOD-TALK WITHOUT GOD-ACT IS OUTRAGEOUS NONSENSE."
> JAMES 2:17 (MSG)

BACKROAD DRIVIN'

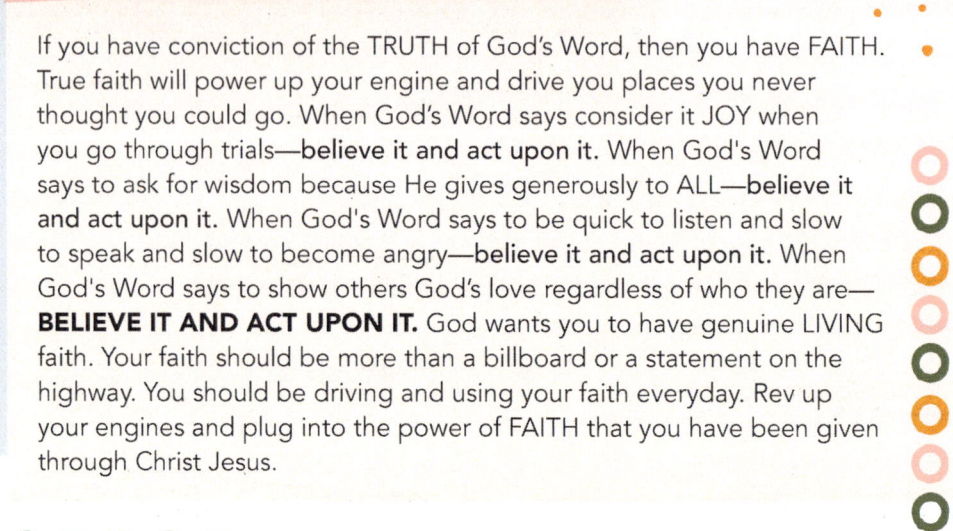

If you have conviction of the TRUTH of God's Word, then you have FAITH. True faith will power up your engine and drive you places you never thought you could go. When God's Word says consider it JOY when you go through trials—**believe it and act upon it**. When God's Word says to ask for wisdom because He gives generously to ALL—**believe it and act upon it**. When God's Word says to be quick to listen and slow to speak and slow to become angry—**believe it and act upon it**. When God's Word says to show others God's love regardless of who they are—**BELIEVE IT AND ACT UPON IT.** God wants you to have genuine LIVING faith. Your faith should be more than a billboard or a statement on the highway. You should be driving and using your faith everyday. Rev up your engines and plug into the power of FAITH that you have been given through Christ Jesus.

ADDITIONAL SIGHTSEEING

Look up Ephesians 3:12, Colossians 1:23, 1 Timothy 4:12, and Galatians 3:26

The Bible has A LOT to say about faith! What do these Scriptures say? (Answers on bottom)

Ephesians 3:12

Colossians 1:23

1 Timothy 4:12

Galatians 3:26

1. In faith, we may approach God with freedom and confidence. 2. Faith gives us strength. 3. Faith sets an example for other believers. 4. We are called daughters of God because of our faith in Jesus.

STOP and write down your prayers.

Lord,

I pray that I have living faith this week. Porsches were meant to have powerful engines, and I was meant to have faith with action. Drive with me, direct my steps, and teach me to believe with FAITH and action!

Amen.

James 2:14-18

JAMES 2:19-24

WHERE THE RUBBER MEETS THE ROAD

"You believe that there is one God. Good! Even the demons believe that—and shudder. You foolish man, do you want evidence that faith without deeds is useless? Was not our ancestor Abraham considered **righteous** for what he did when he offered his son Isaac on the altar? You see that his faith and his actions were working together, and his faith was made complete by what he did. And the scripture was fulfilled that says,'Abraham believed God, and it was credited to him as **righteousness**,' and he was called God's friend. You see that a person is justified by what he does and not by faith alone."

DEFINITION: Righteousness

1. free from guilt or sin, upright, just, straight, innocent, true, sincere

DISCUSSION

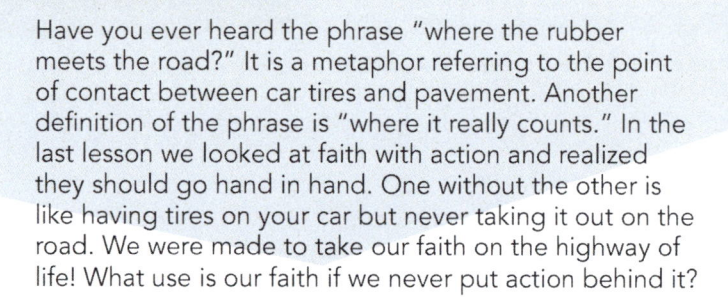

Have you ever heard the phrase "where the rubber meets the road?" It is a metaphor referring to the point of contact between car tires and pavement. Another definition of the phrase is "where it really counts." In the last lesson we looked at faith with action and realized they should go hand in hand. One without the other is like having tires on your car but never taking it out on the road. We were made to take our faith on the highway of life! What use is our faith if we never put action behind it?

Katie did NOT want to write the note. After all, why should she? She had not hurt anyone. It was Morgan that hurt Katie with her sarcastic comments. However, as time went on, her hurtful words grew into bitterness, anger, and judgment. Katie knew God wanted her to show Morgan the same mercy that Christ had shown her—but this was NOT as easy as it sounded. Deep in her heart, Katie knew she needed to sit down and write Morgan a letter. The next day, she slipped the note into Morgan's locker and said a quick prayer, "OK Lord, I did what you told me to do. I pray that our friendship is healed. Thank You for being so faithful to me."

That night Katie got a phone call from Morgan. Morgan had no idea

how her words had hurt Katie, and she asked her for forgiveness. By the end of the conversation, Katie could feel her anger lift and in its place was laughter and renewed faith.

When we put action behind our faith, it increases our trust in God and sets an example for others. Faith is like a muscle and the more we use it, the stronger we get. Remember James 1:3 where it says that perseverance must finish its work to make us complete? Perseverance, often called patience, is developing the COMPLETENESS AND MATURITY we need during the trials of life. **Following God's Road Signs**, even when it isn't easy, is exactly where the rubber meets the road. Let's take our FAITH on the highway of LIFE!

DIRECTIONAL QUESTIONS

1. What does it mean to be righteous? Why was Abraham considered righteous?

2. Do you know the story of Abraham and Isaac? Read Genesis 22:3-14.

3. How did Abraham's faith and actions work together? What did Abraham BELIEVE God would do (Gen. 22:8,14)?

4. Our FAITH in God is like a muscle. The more we exercise it, the stronger we get. When have you put action behind your faith and exercised this spiritual muscle?

" OFFERING ISSAC ON THE ALTAR WAS THE HARDEST TEST ABRAHAM EVER FACED, BUT HE CAME THROUGH VICTORIOUSLY BECAUSE HE TRUSTED IN GOD." -WARREN WIERSBE

BACKROAD DRIVIN'

ABRAHAM believed that God would provide—NO MATTER WHAT! His faith was so STRONG that it is recorded in James and provides an example for us. Trials are real, and we need to be ready when they come. Just like the athlete prepares for the race, we need to be prepared for the trials of life. When you BELIEVE in God, study the Bible, and exercise your faith, you are training for the BIG RACE. Abraham is one of your top coaches! We learn from him that when FAITH and ACTION work together, our faith in God is strengthened, our trust in God is strengthened, and we are being made complete by our obedience. When trials come, this IS "where the rubber meets the road." This is when you ask yourself, "Do I really believe in all this? Do I really believe that God will provide in my situation? Does He really care about me?" When it REALLY counts, buckle up in God's car and drive with FAITH and ACTION.

ADDITIONAL SIGHTSEEING

Look up Deuteronomy 31:6, Joshua 1:9, and Psalm 34:17-18

When you act in faith, God promises to always be with you. What do these Scriptures say about the promise of HIS presence? (Answers on bottom)

Deuteronomy 31:6

Joshua 1:9

Psalm 34:17-18

God promises 1. never to leave you nor forsake you. 2. that He will be with you wherever you go. 3. The Lord hears us when we cry out to Him, and He delivers us from our troubles.

STOP and write down your prayers.

Lord,

I pray that I will put faith behind my actions this week. It's one thing to believe and another to live out that BELIEF. Develop in me the FAITH and ACTION I need to finish the race of life so I can end with righteousness!

Amen.

James 2:19-24

JAMES 2:25-26

NO MATTER THE MAKE OR MODEL

"In the same way, was not Rahab the harlot also **justified** by works when she received the messengers and sent them out by another way? For just as the body without the spirit is dead, so also faith without works is dead." (NASB)

DEFINITION: Justified
1. to demonstrate or prove to be just, right, or valid
2. to declare free of blame; absolve

DISCUSSION

Rahab was a prostitute. How could God use someone for His purposes who made so many bad choices? God knew Rahab's heart. He knew that she feared HIM AND WANTED to change. Haven't we ALL made bad choices in our lives? Sometimes we think that God wouldn't dare use someone like us—**but He CAN and He WILL.**

Reilly couldn't move. She knew this youth ski trip was a BIG mistake. How could God even begin to love someone like her? She had made WAY too many bad choices and KNEW God was shaking His head in shame, just the way her parents did. Now it was time for kids to make a personal confession of Christ. "NO WAY," she thought. "I am NOT going down there. Besides, everyone will laugh if they saw me." But deep in her heart, Reilly sensed a change. Maybe God really DID love her just the way she was. Maybe God really DID forgive her when Jesus died. She thought only good kids shared in God's love, but perhaps her thinking was wrong from the beginning. With her heart pounding and her palms sweating, she slowly got up from her seat and walked down to the front of the room. In her heart, she prayed, "I do believe in you God, and I want a new beginning."

We have looked at two very different characters in the Bible who demonstrated **trust and action** over **fear and disobedience**—Abraham and Rahab. It is important to understand that God loves ALL of His children equally. He desires for all of us to be a part of HIS Kingdom. It doesn't matter the make, or model, the color of your skin, your past decisions, or future plans . . . GOD wants YOU! The world will whisper in your ear that you are not good enough, but God says that is a lie. His son died for ALL, showing no favoritism. He did this so that you may be **justified**—made right and free from your sin. You are declared a daughter of the KING when you believe in Jesus!

DIRECTIONAL QUESTIONS

1. Do you know the BRAVE story of Rahab? Read Joshua 2:1-21.

2. What did Rahab do with the Israelite spies (vs. 4,6)? What did she believe about God (vs. 9-11)? What did the spies promise her (vs. 17-19)?

3. How did Rahab's faith and actions work together?

4. Do you feel sometimes you are not good enough to be a part of God's plan? How does Rahab's story encourage you?

"GOD IS VERY GOOD IN MAKING LEMONADE OUT OF LEMONS"

BACKROAD DRIVIN'

Rahab's faith is mentioned in both Hebrews and James. She is a true hero because she hid the men Joshua sent as spies and trusted in God against all odds. In Joshua 6:22-23, the two spies rescued Rahab and her family the day that Jericho was attacked. Remember the story of Joshua marching around the city seven times and the walls "came a crashin' down?" That day, Rahab the prostitute was saved because of her obedience and FAITH in God. Did you know that she is also mentioned in the lineage of Jesus? YES! In Matthew 1:5, Rahab is mentioned as the wife of Salmon and the mother of Boaz. We do not know for sure, but some scholars speculate that Salmon could have been one of the spies. Rahab's entire life was turned around and used by God because she combined her FAITH with ACTION. Rahab chose to trust, leave her past behind, and be made new. No matter the make or model, **God's GRACE is sufficient for all.**

ADDITIONAL SIGHTSEEING

Look up 2 Corinthians 5:17, Isaiah 43:18, Ezekiel 36:26, and Psalm 51:10

God's grace and forgiveness is available to ALL who believe—regardless of your past mistakes. If you are willing, He CAN and WILL use you. What do these verses say about being made new in Jesus Christ?

2 Corinthians 5:17

Isaiah 43:18

Ezekiel 36:26

Psalm 51:10

1. In Jesus, we are a NEW creation, the OLD is gone and the new has come. 2. We should not dwell on the past. 3. God will give you a new heart and a new spirit. 4. When we pray for a new heart, God will give us a steadfast spirit.

STOP
and write down your prayers.

Lord,

I know that no matter what decisions I have made in the past, You can make them right when I believe in Your Son, Jesus. Your grace is perfect to cover all my past mistakes, and You can use me to lead others to you! Thank You for Your amazing GRACE.

Amen.

James 2:25-26

JAMES 2:1-26

Artist Workshop Ahead

THE HEART ART

"But the things that come out of the mouth come from the HEART..." Matthew 15:18

HOW TO:

1. Cut out two 12 x 12 inches pieces of burlap and lay on top of each other.

2. Using heart template, trace 1/2 of the heart using chalk. Flip your template to the other side to complete your heart and cut. You will be cutting through two pieces.

3. Hot glue the two pieces together leaving a one-inch border. DO NOT glue the bottom 1/4 of your heart.

4. Stuff your heart with paper and glue the remaining edges.

5. Using white paint, paint a heart onto the burlap using a foam brush.

6. Twist strips of fabric into flowers (demonstrated in art video) and glue onto your heart using a low-temp glue gun.

7. Cut wire and thread through the burlap to make a hanger. Coil the ends of the wire and embellish with beads.

8. Print out the Heart Art Scripture and add to your heart with wire.

ART SUPPLIES:

- (2) 12 x 12 inches Square of Burlap
- Low-Temp Hot Glue Gun and Glue Sticks
- White Paint
- Foam Brush
- 2 x 12 inch strips of assorted colored fabric (about eight)
- Clipboard (optional)
- Chalk
- Scissors
- Wire (26-28 guage)
- Cross, Beads, Embellishment, etc.
- Scripture and Heart Template
- Paper

DOWNLOAD THE HEART ART VIDEO and TEMPLATES @ **thouartexalted.com/James-art**

The password is:
GREEN LIGHT

- **Chapter Two Overview:** Don't show Favoritism. Love your neighbor as yourself. Mercy TRIUMPHS over judgment. Faith without action is DEAD.

James tells us that pure religion is loving your neighbor as yourself and showing the same mercy to others that Christ showed us. Pure religion is not being polluted by the world or showing favoritism or judgment. The second chapter of James can be summed up by looking into our hearts. Matthew 15:18 says, "But the things that come out of the mouth come from the **HEART.**" Remember the lesson that mentioned our hearts need daily maintenance? If our heart is full of judgment, guess what comes out of our mouth? You got it . . . pollution! God wants us to be **merciful** and loving. Let's fill our hearts with genuine faith. That's what the Heart Art is ALL about!

JAMES 3:1-6

COOL DOWN THE RADIATOR!

"Not many of you should presume to be teachers, my brothers, because you know that we who teach will be judged more strictly. We ALL stumble in many ways. If anyone is never at fault in what he says, he is a perfect man, able to keep his whole body in check. When we put bits into the mouths of horses to make them obey us, we can turn the whole animal. Or take ships as an example. Although they are so large and are driven by strong winds, they are steered by a very small rudder wherever the pilot wants to go. Likewise the tongue is a small part of the body, but it makes great **boasts.** Consider what a great forest is set on fire by a small spark. The tongue also is a fire, a world of evil among the parts of the body. It corrupts the whole person, sets the whole course of his life on fire, and is itself set on fire by hell."

DEFINITION: Boast

1. to glorify oneself in speech; talk in a self-admiring way, to BRAG

DISCUSSION

We ALL make mistakes, don't we? How many times has our tongue gotten us into a heap of trouble? James has already told us that God wants us to be QUICK to listen, yet SLOW to speak (James 1:19). Why? James knew that even though the tongue is small, it controls the whole body. Just a quick comment can start a HUGE fire!

I NEVER should have told her that. The very second it left my mouth, I wished I could have put it back. I told Helen that Keith was adorable. He was cute, smart, and I really liked him. But the next thing I knew, our little secret was all over school. Really? I thought Helen could be trusted. Now our friendship is ruined. I am so frustrated and not to mention completely EMBARRASSED. How could something so small be made into such a HUGE ordeal? I'll never tell her anything again.

Have you ever tried to put toothpaste back into the tube? It's impossible! It's also just as tricky to take back the words you say—especially when they are mean, manipulative, or that you do NOT want repeated. **The tongue is a powerful part of the body.** In fact, James believed that if we can control the tongue, then we can control our entire body. Today's lesson is called "Cool Down the Radiator." Radiators can get overheated, just like us! But instead of coolant, we need to take God's advice and be CAREFUL with what we say. THINK before you speak, be quick to listen, and remember to add some coolant to your tongue!

DIRECTIONAL QUESTIONS

1. Who is (was) your favorite teacher? Why?

2. Why do you think James is telling us that teachers will be judged more strictly?

3. How does the tongue affect the whole body? Has your tongue ever gotten you in trouble? Have you ever needed to add some coolant?

4. What are the three images used to describe the tongue? Can you relate to any of these ideas?

"IF YOU CAN'T SAY ANYTHING NICE, DON'T SAY IT AT ALL." -MOM

BACKROAD DRIVIN'

A TEACHER is someone with great influence. Teachers have the ability to convince, instruct, and open up our minds to amazing truths and ideas. But, there is also a HUGE responsibility that comes with teaching—not to mention GREAT accountability from God's perspective. The greatest teacher we have is Jesus. He used His tongue with wisdom and purpose. Jesus did not BOAST or BRAG for His own glory, but instead used His speech to glorify and TEACH us about GOD. Jesus surrendered His plan many times to complete the mission for which He was sent—to save the world from sin and teach us how to have a personal relationship with His Father. He taught us how to live under trying circumstances, how to love one another, and how to TALK with grace and encouragement. Jesus is the BEST example we have . . . using His TONGUE for PRAISE and not for pride.

ADDITIONAL SIGHTSEEING

Look up Psalm 19:14, Romans 12:6-8, 1 Timothy 6:3-5, and 2 Timothy 3:16-17

God has a lot to say about teaching and using our tongue with wisdom and purpose. What do you find from the following Scriptures? (Answers on bottom)

Psalm 19:14

Romans 12:6-8

1 Timothy 6:3-5

2 Timothy 3:16-17

1. God wants the words of our mouths and the "thoughts" of our hearts to be pleasing to HIM. 2. Teaching is a GIFT. 3. False teachers are conceited and understand NOTHING—they have unhealthy interests. 4. ALL Scripture is useful for TEACHING.

STOP and write down your prayers.

Lord,

I know how my tongue can get me into trouble—FAST. I pray You will be my teacher and that You will help me to control my speech. I pray NOT to brag but to only glorify You in what I say and how I behave. Thank You Lord for being my Teacher!

Amen.

James 3:1-6

JAMES 3:7-12

NO DIESEL FUEL IN AN UNLEADED ENGINE!

"All kinds of animals, birds, reptiles and sea creatures are being tamed and have been tamed by mankind, but no human being can tame the tongue. It is a restless evil, full of deadly **poison.** With the tongue we praise our Lord and Father, and with it we curse human beings, who have been made in God's likeness. Out of the same mouth come praise and cursing. My brothers and sisters, this should not be. Can both fresh water and salt water flow from the same spring? My brothers and sisters, can a fig tree bear olives, or a grapevine bear figs? Neither can a salt spring produce fresh water."

DEFINITION: Poison

1. a substance that causes injury, illness, or death
2. something destructive or fatal, to kill or harm with poison.
3. to pollute, to have a harmful influence on; corrupt

DISCUSSION

Do you know what would happen if you put diesel fuel in an unleaded tank? It would ruin the engine. In this case, it would poison the car. The same is true with our tongue. James tells us that our words can be full of deadly poison. We talked about pollution in James 1:26 (Walk the Talk) when James tells us that our religion is worth nothing if we can't keep a tight reign on our tongue. Today we will see that our speech can be poisonous. This little muscle can praise one minute and then curse the next.

"That was a fantastic sermon!" Hannah thought to herself. She was excited about church again. Hanna desired to study God's Word, and she was learning something NEW each Sunday. Today's sermon was titled "Encouragement and Building One Another Up!" Hannah's spirit was soaring until the server at lunch messed up her order. "Really? How could you mess up such a simple order? I did NOT want cheese, mustard, or pickles! All I want is a plain burger with just ketchup. Geez Louise!" Had she really said it? Was she that judgmental to the waitress who was taking her order? One minute

Hannah was filled with God's Spirit and the next she was filled with a destructive tongue — complaining about mustard!

Can you relate to this story? One minute you are praising and the next you are cursing. The Bible teaches us how to live, how to be an example for others, and how to use our speech for God's purposes. Yes, the tongue can be poisonous, but it can also be a powerful tool for praise! Let's not mix unleaded with diesel.

DIRECTIONAL QUESTIONS

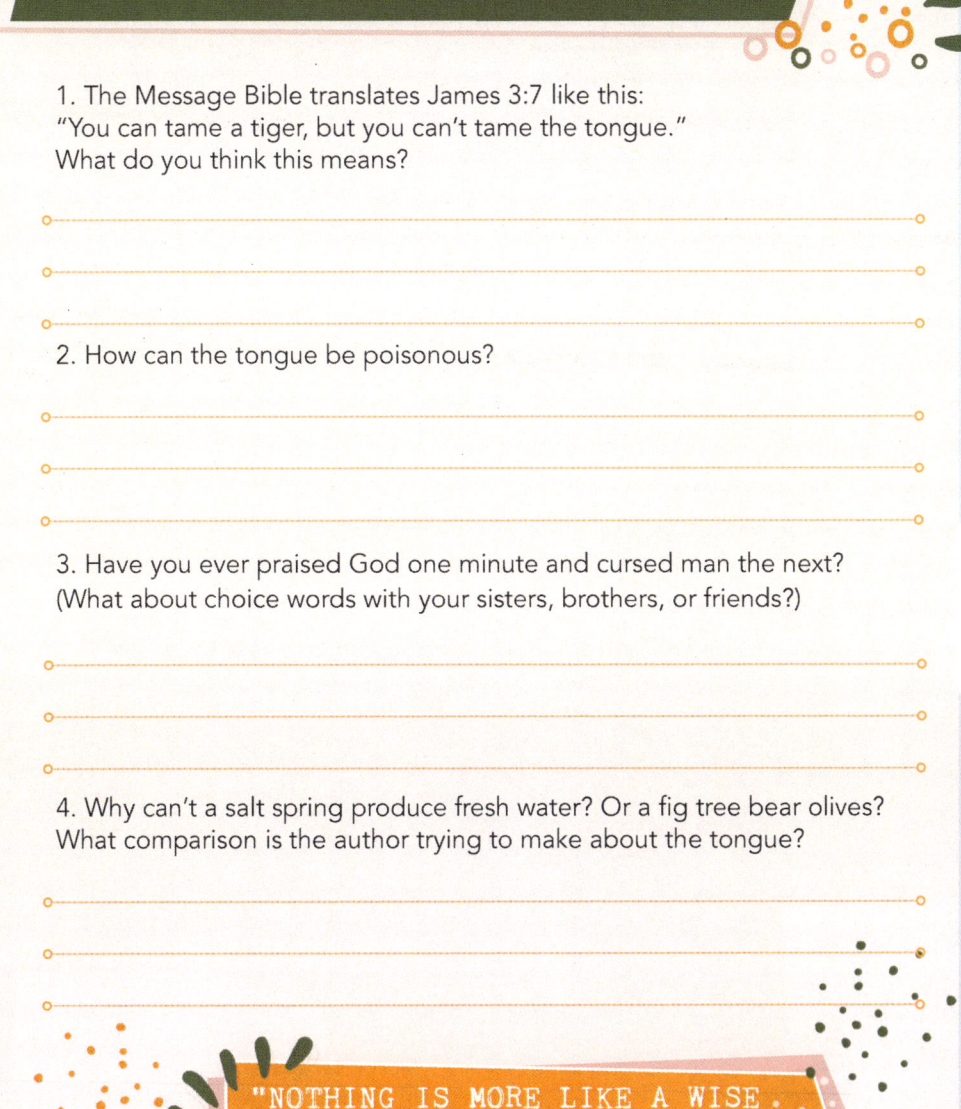

1. The Message Bible translates James 3:7 like this:
"You can tame a tiger, but you can't tame the tongue."
What do you think this means?

2. How can the tongue be poisonous?

3. Have you ever praised God one minute and cursed man the next? (What about choice words with your sisters, brothers, or friends?)

4. Why can't a salt spring produce fresh water? Or a fig tree bear olives? What comparison is the author trying to make about the tongue?

> "NOTHING IS MORE LIKE A WISE MAN THAN A FOOL WHO HOLDS HIS TONGUE." -FRANCIS DE SALES

BACKROAD DRIVIN'

The Bible describes the tongue as being deceitful, reckless, and harsh. It also acknowledges that the tongue can be used for wisdom, healing, and gentleness. This little muscle has a lot of power! The real choice becomes ours. How are you going to control your tongue and use it for the good purposes it was intended? The answer lies in Scripture.

> **Luke 6:45** "The good man brings good things out of the good stored up in his heart, and the evil man brings evil things out of the evil stored up in his heart. For out of the OVERFLOW of his heart his mouth speaks."

> **Ephesians 4:29** "Do not let any unwholesome (harmful) talk come out of your mouths but only what is helpful for building others up according to their needs, that it may benefit those who listen."

Luke believed that what we say reflects what is happening in our hearts and the Ephesians text reminds us to use words ONLY that will help others. This is the perfect picture of adding unleaded fuel to an unleaded engine—or adding God's Word to a Godly heart.

ADDITIONAL SIGHTSEEING

Look up James 1:19-20, Ephesians 5:4,19-20, Psalm 34:13, and Colossians 4:6

What does God say about the tongue? (Answers on bottom)

James 1:19-20

_____

_____

Ephesians 5:4,19-20

_____

_____

Psalm 34:13

_____

_____

Colossians 4:6

_____

_____

1. We should be quick to listen and slow to speak. 2. No foolish talking but rather thanksgiving. 3. Keep your tongue from evil and lies. 4. Your conversations need to be full of grace.

STOP
and write down your prayers.

Lord,

Teach me how to speak with encouragement, grace, and wisdom. I pray to fill my heart with YOUR words so that my tongue may overflow with love toward others.

Amen.

James 3:7-12

JAMES 3:13-18

THE DIVINE DRIVER'S MANUAL

"Who is wise and understanding among you? Let him show it by his good life, by deeds done in the humility that comes from **wisdom**. But if you harbor bitter envy and selfish ambition in your hearts, do not boast about it or deny the truth. Such "wisdom" does not come down from heaven but is earthly, unspiritual, of the devil. For where you have envy and selfish ambition, there you find disorder and every evil practice. But the wisdom that comes from heaven is first of all pure; then peace-loving, considerate, submissive, full of mercy and good fruit, impartial and sincere. Peacemakers who sow in peace raise a harvest of righteousness."

DEFINITION: Wisdom

1. knowledge of what is true or right coupled with just judgment as to action; discernment, or insight

DISCUSSION

When you start driving, one of the first things you should read is the DRIVER'S MANUAL. This handbook will teach you the right way to drive vs. the wrong and careless way to drive. The Bible is very similar. God, our driving instructor, has gone to great measures to provide the BEST handbook there is to life. This passage in the DIVINE DRIVER'S MANUAL defines two types of wisdom: earthly wisdom and heavenly wisdom.

Rachel really wanted to ask Scotty to the Valentine's dance. But Rachel knew that her good friend Allie wanted to ask him, too. But if she got to History class early enough, she could beat Allie to it. After all, Allie had not even mentioned the dance or asking Scotty in about a week. This was Rachel's chance. But something inside her knew that her decision was selfish. Should she go ahead and act on impulse or take some time to talk with Allie? She knew deep down that she was jealous of Allie and the way everything seemed so easy for her. Well, not this time. The bell rang and Rachel rushed to History.

Rachel did not have the best intentions, did she? READING the DRIVER'S manual was not her first priority! When we make decisions out of selfish motives, we better expect disorder to follow. God says that true **wisdom** is pure, sincere, considerate, and peace-loving. Are we taking the time to *Follow GOD's Road Signs* for WISDOM or are we making quick decisions that satisfy our own agenda? Earthly wisdom is "having it your way"—often at the expense of others. Heavenly wisdom is taking God's advice and reading the manual!

DIRECTIONAL QUESTIONS

1. How do we show our wisdom according to this passage?

2. Making a list, compare and contrast the two kinds of wisdom.

3. Why do you think humility plays such an important role in heavenly wisdom?

4. What is the result of earthly wisdom? What is the result of heavenly wisdom? What are ways you can develop wisdom from above?

> "TWISTING THE TRUTH TO MAKE YOURSELVES SOUND WISE ISN'T WISDOM." JAMES 3:13 (MSG)

BACKROAD DRIVIN'

HUMILITY plays a huge role in having heavenly wisdom. Why? Because when we are humble, we are NOT putting ourselves first. Remember the lesson about loving our neighbors as ourselves? (James 2:8, No Traffic Violation) The Message Bible says, "Live well, live wisely, live humbly. It's the way you live, not the way you talk, that counts. Mean-spirited ambition isn't wisdom." Wisdom does not equal how smart you are, how much material wealth you do or do not have, or your social standing with your friends. "Real wisdom, God's wisdom, begins with a holy life and is characterized by getting along with others. It is gentle and reasonable, overflowing with mercy and blessings, not hot one day and cold the next, not two-faced" (James 3:17, MSG). **Here is a challenge.** Write down the two descriptions of wisdom and put them in your room. When you wake up in the morning, ask God to give you a tongue that glorifies HIM and wisdom that will be rooted in humility and peace. When you live out each day in peace, you will be on the right road with God, following the Divine Driver's Manual.

ADDITIONAL SIGHTSEEING

Look up Psalm 111:10, Proverbs 4:6-7, Proverbs 13:10, and Proverbs 16:16

What do these verses teach us about God's wisdom? (Answers on bottom)

Psalm 111:10

Proverbs 4:6-7

Proverbs 13:10

Proverbs 16:16

1. The beginning of wisdom is to fear (respect) the Lord. 2. Wisdom will protect you and watch over you. 3. Wisdom is found by taking good advice. 4. Wisdom is richer than gold or silver.

STOP
and write down your prayers.

Lord,

Teach me to LIVE WELL, LIVE WISELY, and LIVE HUMBLY. When I get off the road and stumble in my own wisdom, remind me that only YOUR wisdom can bear good fruit and bring about peace. I want Your wisdom so that I can be overflowing in mercy and love.

Amen.

James 3:13-18

JAMES 3:1-18

Artist Workshop Ahead

FAITH BANNER

THE FAITH banner

"...I will show you my FAITH by what I do." — James 2:18 FAITH without ACTION is dead...

HOW TO:

1. Begin by gluing strips of fabric and paper to your canvas. The strips should be 2 to 3 inches wide and 10 inches long.

2. While your glue is drying, cut out your cross and butterflies (template can be downloaded online).

3. Using a glue stick, gently (not using a lot of glue) glue your cross, leaves, and butterflies onto your paper.

4. Using a pallate or plastic knife, spread white spackle over your whole canvas. Hint: Use strokes that push away from the template. This prevents spackle from getting underneath.

5. Carefully peel up your cross, leaves, and butterflies exposing the bottom color.

6. When dry, add trim, buttons, or ribbon to top and bottom on banner.

7. Bend pop tops slightly to form an angle. Hot glue flat part onto the back of your canvas (1" from top and sides). Repeat on other side. Thred fabric through the holes of pop top to make a "handle." Tie off fabric on canvas side.

8. Add Scripture circle with yarn, twine, or wire. Attach to the fabric handle.

ART SUPPLIES:

- Canvas 10 x 10
- Scrapbook Paper/ Fabric
- Low-Temp Hot Glue Gun and Glue Sticks
- Trim: Pom Pom, Ribbon, Yarn
- Kitchen Twine or Wire
- Embellishments: Buttons
- Glue Stick
- Scissors
- Template of Cross and Butterflies
- Faith Banner Circle
- Printer and Cardstock Paper
- 2 Pop Tops (top of soda can)
- Fabric Strip (2' x 2")

DOWNLOAD THE FAITH BANNER VIDEO and TEMPLATES
@ **thouartexalted.com/James-art**

The password is:
GREEN LIGHT

The Faith Banner is an important project in our journey of studying **James: Following God's Road Signs.** Our FAITH should be a reflection of HIM. Let's take our FAITH on the highway of life!

- **Chapter Three Overview:** Don't presume to be a teacher because those who teach will be judged more strictly. The tongue is a small part of the body, but it makes great boasts. We praise the Father and curse men. Wisdom is two-fold: earthly and Godly. Earthly wisdom is full of disorder and evil, and Godly wisdom is pure, peace-loving, considerate, submissive, full of mercy and good fruit, impartial, and sincere. Peacemakers will sow a harvest of righteousness.

JAMES 4:1-3

LOOKING UNDER THE HOOD OF EARTHLY WISDOM

"What is causing the QUARRELS and fights among you? Don't they come from the evil desires at war within you? You want what you don't have, so you scheme and kill to get it. You are jealous of what others have, but you can't get it, so you fight and wage war to take it away from them. Yet you don't have what you want because you don't ask God for it. And even when you ask, you don't get it because your motives are all wrong—you want only what will give you pleasure." (NLT)

DEFINITION: Quarrels

1. a dispute, an argument
2. a war, a fight, a battle

DISCUSSION

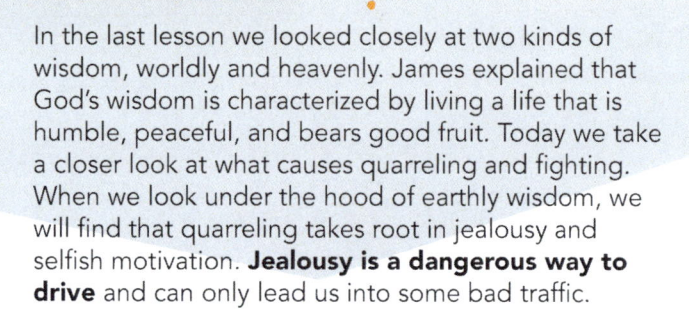

In the last lesson we looked closely at two kinds of wisdom, worldly and heavenly. James explained that God's wisdom is characterized by living a life that is humble, peaceful, and bears good fruit. Today we take a closer look at what causes quarreling and fighting. When we look under the hood of earthly wisdom, we will find that quarreling takes root in jealousy and selfish motivation. **Jealousy is a dangerous way to drive** and can only lead us into some bad traffic.

Kate had had enough of her big sister. Becca was always accusing her of being mean, taking things out of her room, and not doing her chores. But THIS was the icing on the cake. Becca blamed Kate for taking AND losing the watch she had gotten for Christmas. Becca was furious. You could hear the evil words coming from her mouth and you could almost see the fumes coming out of her head. THIS WAS WAR! But Kate was innocent. She had not taken her sister's watch. Becca was being selfish and accusing Kate of something she did not do. Becca's motives were to get Kate in BIG TROUBLE. What should she do? The last thing she wanted was another fight with her sister.

Becca's motives were all wrong. She falsely accused her little sister for taking her watch when the responsibility was hers alone. Quarreling is often caused by the evil desires we have inside our own hearts. In the last lesson we studied that peacemakers who sow in peace raise a harvest of righteousness. When we are jealous and fighting, we are not sowing peace—we are planting our own selfish motives, resulting in "disorder and every evil practice" (James 3:16). **Quarreling is a car wreck waiting to happen.** Focus on the road and follow God's direction for wisdom.

DIRECTIONAL QUESTIONS

1. What causes quarreling and fights among you, with your friends, parents, or siblings?

___

2. What are the "evil desires" that are at war within you?

___

3. Have you ever been jealous of something someone else had? How did you handle it?

___

4. Why do you think motives are so important when you are seeking wisdom from God?

___

"THE WARS AMONG US ARE CAUSED BY THE WARS WITHIN US" -WARREN WIERSBE

BACKROAD DRIVIN'

Selfishness is the gas that fuels jealousy, and **jealousy is the gas that fuels quarreling and fighting.** We have learned in James that what goes on in the inside will be reflected on the outside. The desires of our hearts will overflow into our everyday lives. If we are self-centered and judgmental, we will reflect favoritism, actions without faith, anger, and a sour tongue. If we are God-centered, we will reflect joy, mercy, loving others as ourselves, peace, righteousness, and godly wisdom. Evil desires are just that—EVIL. Quarreling and fighting are NEON signs of the selfishness growing in our hearts. When our desire to WANT something overrides our desire to wait and listen for God's direction, we should expect quarreling and fighting. Why? Because when our goal is to GET WHAT we WANT when we WANT, God is out of the equation. We are operating in selfish motivation. God wants us to make decisions that will reflect His character, but He will never MAKE us. The choice is ours. We have the freedom to choose which hood to look under—the hood of earthly wisdom or the hood of Godly wisdom. I pray you choose God's.

ADDITIONAL SIGHTSEEING

Look up Romans 2:8, Proverbs 18:1, 1 Corinthians 13:4-6, and Philippians 2:1-4

What do these verses teach you about selfishness? (Answers on bottom)

Romans 2:8

Proverbs 18:1

1 Corinthians 13:4-6

Philippians 2:1-4

1. Those who are self-seeking will experience wrath and anger. 2. Selfishness defies all sound judgment. 3. Love is not selfish. 4. Being like-minded in Christ is not being selfish.

STOP
and write down your prayers.

Lord,

I pray that when I sense quarreling and fighting in my spirit that I will quickly examine my heart and my motives. I pray to ask You for Your wisdom and not seek my personal agenda. I pray to be a reflection of YOU!

Amen.

James 4:1-3

JAMES 4:4-6

STOP, RIGHT TURN ONLY!

"You **adulterous** people, don't you know that friendship with the world means enmity against God? Therefore, anyone who chooses to be a friend of the world becomes an enemy of God. Or do you think Scripture says without reason that he jealously longs for the spirit he has caused to dwell in us? But he gives us more grace. That is why Scripture says: 'God opposes the proud but shows favor to the humble.'"

DEFINITION: Adulterous

1. The Hebrew definition is being faithless toward God: ungodly, to act dishonestly, to deceive; marital unfaithfulness

DISCUSSION

In this lesson, we see the word jealousy pop up again! In the last lesson, jealousy was caught up in quarreling and selfish motivation. Here we discover a different kind of jealously—God's jealousy toward us, His children. God is our Creator, and He gets pretty jealous when we desire other things over Him. In fact, when we choose worldly characteristics over Godly ones, The Message Bible says, "We are cheating on Him." Really? Can you imagine cheating on GOD? That's strong language.

Angela and Luke had been dating each other since eighth grade. But lately, Luke was acting strange. He didn't seem as interested in Angela's funny stories the plans for the weekend. This all made sense when Angela found out the truth. While she was on Spring Break with her family, Luke started hanging out with Caroline. Angela was embarrassed and angry. He CHEATED on her! She HAD to admit, she was jealous. Why would Luke chose Caroline over her? His deception hurt to the core.

In the Bible, God's relationship with us is often symbolized by a marriage relationship. We are the bride, and He is the groom. By making choices that are of "the world," we compromise our relationship with God. In studying James, we see that doubt, pride, deception, favoritism, gossip, false religion, judgment, and selfish ambition are many of the ways we can choose being "friends with this world." **Following God's Road Signs** means taking the RIGHT TURNS in life. Let's not cheat on God and take wrong turns. He is JEALOUS for us with a Godly jealousy. The Message Bible says, "What God gives in love is far better than anything else you will find" (James 4:6).

DIRECTIONAL QUESTIONS

1. What do you think it means to have friendship with the world? Why would this be enmity or hostile toward God?

2. How would you describe the jealousy God has toward you?

3. Be honest: do you have more of a relationship with God or the world?

4. Why would God oppose the proud and show favor to the humble? What does this have to do with giving us, His children, MORE GRACE?

> "IF YOU BELIEVE IN THE BIBLE, YOU WILL DO WHAT IT SAYS."
> -RICK WARREN

BACKROAD DRIVIN'

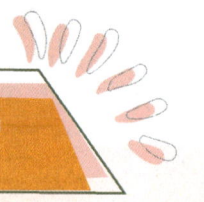

James 4:6 says God's Spirit lives in us and that He gives us **more grace.** Why would God give His children more grace when we often choose to go the ways of the world? That seems like opposite thinking, right? Let's take a closer look at the text because it's FULL of opposites! Do you see them? Crazy enough, an opposite of GRACE is ENMITY, a feeling of hostility. When we choose to be friends with the world, **we choose to be hostile toward God.** The opposite of humility is pride—a high opinion of one's own importance. When we choose to be prideful, **we choose to be more important than God.** Is God showing us opposites to teach us to STOP, address our direction, and CHOOSE to take the right turns He desires? By adding MORE Grace, God shows us an extra outpouring of His loving kindness when we least deserve or expect it. Why would He do this? Because His Spirit lives IN US, and He is jealous FOR US—eager to protect what is precious to Him. He is jealous for our attention, our devotion, our time, and our salvation. **His love is so great for us that He gives us MORE GRACE.**

ADDITIONAL SIGHTSEEING

Look up Exodus 20:4, Exodus 34:14, 2 Corinthians 11:2, and Deuteronomy 4:23-24

What do these verses teach you about God's jealousy toward you? (Answers on bottom)

Exodus 20:4

Exodus 34:14

2 Corinthians 11:2

Deuteronomy 4:23-24

1. God is a jealous God. We do not serve or bow down to any other god. 2. We do not worship any other god. 3. Our only love is Christ. 4. He is a jealous God, and we are NOT to forget his covenant with us.

STOP
and write down your prayers.

Lord,

I thank You for ALWAYS loving me and giving me MORE grace, even when I don't deserve it. Help me to always choose to be YOUR friend and not the world's. Help me to be humble and serve YOU with all my heart.

Amen.

James 4:4-6

JAMES 4:7-10

YIELD

"**Submit** yourselves, then, to God. Resist the devil, and he will flee from you. Come near to God and he will come near to you. Wash your hands, you sinners, and purify your hearts, you double-minded. Grieve, mourn and wail. Change your laughter to mourning and your joy to gloom. Humble yourselves before the Lord, and he will lift you up."

DEFINITION: Submit

1. to yield or surrender (oneself) to the will or authority or another

DISCUSSION

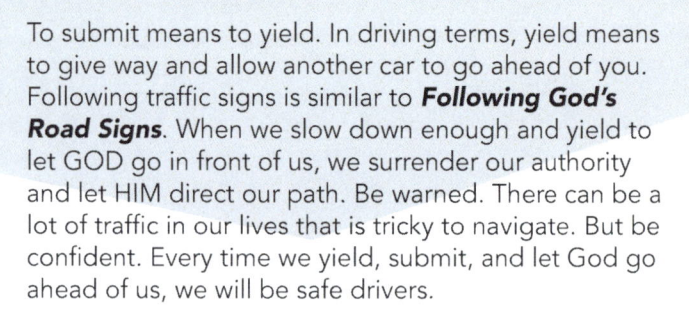

To submit means to yield. In driving terms, yield means to give way and allow another car to go ahead of you. Following traffic signs is similar to **Following God's Road Signs**. When we slow down enough and yield to let GOD go in front of us, we surrender our authority and let HIM direct our path. Be warned. There can be a lot of traffic in our lives that is tricky to navigate. But be confident. Every time we yield, submit, and let God go ahead of us, we will be safe drivers.

The end of the third quarter was getting closer and closer. Daley knew this meant extra quizzes, tests, and of course, Spring Break! Who wants to study when the weather is warm, the flowers are beginning to bloom, and vacation is on the horizon? Her mind began to wander when she realized that softball was about to begin, too. This meant practice every day after school and at least two games a week. Daley felt like she was in a traffic jam and all the horns were honking for her attention. She had a headache just thinking about her schedule. How was she going to juggle all the demands in her life?

Tricky traffic jams and busy schedules. Life can be so overwhelming that we can feel trapped in ALL our activities. James tells us this is the work of the devil whose only desire is for us to crash and burn. But God has another plan! This is why James 4:7-10 is so important for safe driving. We need to YIELD to God, especially when life can be too much for us to navigate. The Message Bible says, "So let God work his will in you. Yell a loud NO to the devil and watch him scamper. Say a quiet YES to God, and he'll be there in no time." God is ready, willing, and waiting for us to CALL out His name. Submit to His plan, YIELD to His direction, and you'll be out of traffic in no time.

DIRECTIONAL QUESTIONS

1. What do you think it means to submit to God?

2. What does "resisting the devil" look like? Why would he flee from you?

3. When James tells us to come near to God, what is the promise when you yield to this invitation? What does that mean to you?

4. How can we humble ourselves before the Lord? (See Backroad Driving)

"GET DOWN ON YOUR KNEES BEFORE THE MASTER; IT'S THE ONLY WAY YOU'LL GET ON YOUR FEET." (MSG)

BACKROAD DRIVIN'

The Message Bible is a great resource that translates biblical text into contemporary language, making it easier for us to understand. In these passages, James tells us that we need to get serious about God—a stark contrast with being friends with the world. He tells us to wake up, resist the devil, and let God work in you! Take a look at these parallel translations.

NIV: "Wash your hands, you sinners, and purify your hearts."
MSG: "Quit dabbling in sin. Purify your inner life. Quit playing the field."

NIV: "Grieve, mourn and wail. Change your laughter to mourning ..."
MSG: "Hit bottom, and cry your eyes out. The fun and games are over. Get serious, really serious."

NIV: "Humble yourselves before the Lord, and he will lift you up."
MSG: "Get down on your knees before the Master; it's the only way you'll get on your feet."

Can you see the benefit of studying two different translations of the Bible? God is clearly telling us to YIELD to His direction, humble ourselves, get on our knees, get serious about Him, and **Follow His Road Signs.**

ADDITIONAL SIGHTSEEING

Look up Romans 12:2, Romans 8:5-9, and 1 John 2:15-17.

God desires us to live for HIM and NOT the world. What does God have to say about living in the world? (Answers on bottom)

Romans 12:2

Romans 8:5-9

1 John 2:15-17

1. Do not be conformed to the patterns of this world. 2. When our minds are focused on the world, we cannot please God. 3. Do not love the world or anything in the world. It will all pass away but the word of God stands forever.

STOP and write down your prayers.

Lord,

I pray this week to yield to Your traffic signs in my life. I pray I would resist the devil and draw closer and closer to You. Purify me, O Lord. Bring me to my knees so that I can worship You with a humble heart.

Amen.

James 4:7-10

JAMES 4:11-17

DEAD END OR NEW BEGINNING?

"Brothers, do not slander one another. Anyone who speaks against his brother or judges him speaks against the law and judges it. When you judge the law, you are not keeping it, but sitting in judgment on it. There is only ONE Lawgiver and Judge, the only one who is able to save and destroy. But you ~ who are you to judge your neighbor? Now listen, you who say, 'Today or tomorrow we will go to this or that city, spend a year there, carry on business and make money.' Why, you do not even know what will happen tomorrow. What is your life? You are a mist that appears for a little while and then **vanishes**. Instead, you ought to say, 'If it is the Lord's will, we will live and do this or that.' As it is, you boast and brag. All such boasting is evil. Anyone, then, who knows the good he ought to do and doesn't do it, sins."

DEFINITION: Vanish

1. disappear suddenly and completely, to pass suddenly from sight

DISCUSSION

As we close chapter four, we see James re-emphasizing specific points he has made all along. Do not judge. Do not say mean things to one another. Listen to the Word, and DO what it says. God is the ONLY judge and He is in control, not us—although we would like to think we are. James is telling us that our life is short, a wisp. So our question is this: **How are you going to live out the gift of life that God, the Creator, has given to you?** Are you going to get serious, like we discussed last week?

The tragedy was terrible. Who would have ever thought it would happen to our school? This is what you see on T.V., not in our own backyard. My Bible study just met that morning where we learned to draw near to God and flee from evil. Now, I am watching my school on national news because of the shooting. Why, Lord? Why would You allow such a senseless crime to happen? One thing I have learned this year is sometimes life doesn't make any sense. But You promise that YOU are close to the broken hearted and save those who are crushed in spirit. I am crushed, Lord. Please come and heal our school.

Tragedy. Life cut short. You might ask yourself if God is really in control. This is a good place to remember to WHOM James is writing. He is writing to believers in Jesus who are being persecuted and perhaps even killed for what they believe. James is reminding them God is the only judge, and we need to live wholeheartedly for HIM. We can make all the plans we want in life, but ultimately, only God knows what the future holds. **Following God's Road Signs** will direct us to the right path, even when life seems like a dead end.

DIRECTIONAL QUESTIONS

1. What are some of the repeated themes in James that you see in these verses? (Hint: the tongue, judgment, actions, faith, etc., . . .)

2. What is the role of a judge? Are you playing judge when you "label" your friends? How about when you boast in your own plans?

3. Have you ever planned something that didn't turn out the way you expected? What was your reaction? Did you TRUST that God might have a different plan or steered you away from making a bad choice?

4. How is boasting in your own plan evil in the eyes of God?

"WE WILL PRAISE HIM IF WE WIN AND WE WILL PRAISE HIM IF WE LOSE. HE WILL GET ALL THE PRAISE." -FACING THE GIANTS

BACKROAD DRIVIN'

OUR PLANS always look promising until life interferes and forces us to make a decision: Is this detour a DEAD END or a NEW BEGINNING? James tells us that our life is just a mist, a vapor. But what does a short life have to do with making plans? Proverbs 19:21 says this:

> "Many are the plans in a man's heart, but it is the Lord's purpose that prevails."

Judgment of one another and planning for tomorrow prove that we are not trusting God's Road Signs. Planning is good, but when you assume the position of control, your plans are only a only a mirage. Proverbs tells us that we can plan, but in the end, God's purpose will TRIUMPH. Remember, God loves us beyond what we could ever imagine! His plan for us is better—we just have to TRUST. Our days are numbered and that is why we should even be more ambitious to live life to the FULLNESS of His glory! God will allow trials in your life often to show you new beginnings. Stop trying to be in control. Look ahead! He offers peace, hope, and direction.

ADDITIONAL SIGHTSEEING

Look up Job 42:2, Proverbs 14:22, Proverbs 21:30, and Isaiah 14:24

What does the Scripture say about God's plans? Your plans? (Answers on bottom)

Job 42:2

Proverbs 14:22

Proverbs 21:30

Isaiah 14:24

1. God's plans can never be stopped. 2. If we plan what is good, we will find love and faithfulness. 3. No plan can succeed against the Lord's plan. 4. Whatever God's purpose and plan is, it will stand.

STOP
and write down your prayers.

Lord,

I know it is good to be organized and to look ahead, but I pray also to understand that YOU are in control of my life. When I come to dead ends, I pray to LOOK for the NEW BEGINNINGS YOU will show me when I follow Your ways and not MY plans.

Amen.

James 4:11-17

JAMES 4:1-17

Artist Workshop Ahead

WISE OLE OWL PILLOW

THE WISE OLE OWL pillow — James 3:17 "But the wisdom that comes from heaven is...PURE..."

HOW TO:

1. Print out the Wise Ole Owl template and Scripture onto cardstock paper.

2. Collect fabrics for your pillow. I used a solid color for the body and a printed pattern for the wings, eyes, etc ...

3. Cut out the pattern for your owl (from printed template) and trace onto the backside of your fabric. Trace two pieces of fabric—one for front and one for back.

4. Cut out, trace remaining pieces, and lay out design.

5. Starting with the body, hot glue the edges leaving the bottom open for stuffing.

6. Stuff body with pillow stuffing and glue opening closed with glue gun.

7. Hot glue remaining parts onto your owl: eyes, fruit, wings, buttons, flower, ribbon, etc.

8. Cut out Scripture and with wire, connect your James Circle Verse onto the ear of your owl pillow.

ART STOP

100

ART SUPPLIES:

- Fabric (both solid and colorful)
- Low-Temp Hot Glue Gun and Glue Sticks
- Scissors
- Owl Template
- Buttons, Ribbon, Fabric Flowers
- Scripture Circle
- Nail for Hole Punch
- Printer and Cardstock Paper
- Pillow Stuffing
- Wire (26-28 guage)

DOWNLOAD THE WISE OLE' OWL VIDEO and TEMPLATES @ **thouartexalted.com/James-art**

The password is:
GREEN LIGHT

- **Chapter Four Review:** Fights and quarrels come from the desires within you. You do not have because you do not ask. Ask with the right motives. A friend of this world is an enemy of God. God gives MORE GRACE. Submit to God and resist the devil. Come NEAR to GOD and He will come NEAR to you. Humble yourselves before the Lord and He WILL lift you up. There is only ONE Judge. Do not boast about tomorrow, instead, ASK God what His will is.

The Wise Ole Owl Project reminds us that heavenly wisdom is about living humbly as we **Follow God's Road Signs**. As a result, our life will be proof of God working in us and we will bear much fruit!

JAMES 5:1-6

BEHAVE BEHIND THE WHEEL

"Now listen, you rich people, weep and wail because of the misery that is coming on you. Your wealth has rotted, and moths have eaten your clothes. Your gold and silver are corroded. Their corrosion will testify against you and eat your flesh like fire. You have hoarded wealth in the last days. Look! The wages you failed to pay the workers who mowed your fields are crying out against you. The cries of the harvesters have reached the ears of the Lord Almighty. You have lived on earth in luxury and **self-indulgence**. You have fattened yourselves in the day of slaughter. You have condemned and murdered the innocent one, who was not opposing you."

DEFINITION: Self-Indulgence

1. excessive indulgence of one's own appetites and desires

DISCUSSION

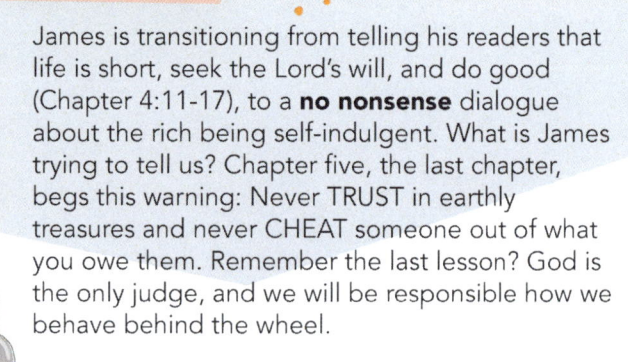

James is transitioning from telling his readers that life is short, seek the Lord's will, and do good (Chapter 4:11-17), to a **no nonsense** dialogue about the rich being self-indulgent. What is James trying to tell us? Chapter five, the last chapter, begs this warning: Never TRUST in earthly treasures and never CHEAT someone out of what you owe them. Remember the last lesson? God is the only judge, and we will be responsible how we behave behind the wheel.

Jenny always wanted a Canon Rebel camera. She dreamed of the day when she would be the BEST photographer on the yearbook staff. Afterall, Jenny thought the staff took sub-par photos. "Not anymore," she thought. "Things are about to change!" Jenny borrowed $200 from her best friend, Amie, and promised to pay her back. She joined the yearbook staff with gusto until her plans of success quickly began to unravel. Amie needed to be paid back for the camera, but Jenny *was not responding to her texts. Amie finally approached Jenny's parents and the truth came out. Jenny didn't have the money. As a result, Jenny's camera was taken away, along with her position on the yearbook staff. She was furious.*

Jenny's self-indulgent attitude left her without a camera and her best friend. Trusting in life's riches and not returning what we borrow can turn our world upside down! It's important to note that the Bible never refers to being rich or having nice things as evil. It becomes evil when we start LOVING money OVER LOVING God. Yes, the things of this earth are attractive, but we must trust that God will give you everything you need.

DIRECTIONAL QUESTIONS

1. In your own words, how would you sum up this passage?

2. Why does our wealth rot? Why do moths eat our clothes? Why does gold and silver corrode? What IS James trying to tell us?

3. Have you ever failed to pay back or give back something you borrowed? Explain.

4. Materially speaking, what do you trust more than God in this world?

"YOU CAN'T TAKE A U-HAUL TO HEAVEN." -BUMPER STICKER

BACKROAD DRIVIN'

The Bible makes it clear that there is a difference between money and the LOVE of money. Take a look at 1 Timothy 6:10. *"For the love of money is a root of all kinds of evil. Some people, eager for money, have wandered from the faith and pierced themselves with many griefs."* Money is NOT the root of all evil, it's the **LOVE** of money. When we become obsessed with our material possessions, our fixation becomes a poison that will destroy our faith. In fact, the word "rust" in this passage is literally translated POISON. Having wealth with the right perspective can be used for God's glory, but when life becomes all about self-indulgence and personal gain, it only leads to destruction. I Timothy 6:17 says this, *"Command those who are rich in this present world not to be arrogant nor to put their hope in wealth, which is so uncertain, but to put their hope in God, who richly provides us with everything for our enjoyment."* Riches will fail us, but our hope in God will not. Behave behind the wheel and trust that GOD's Road Signs will provide us with everything we NEED!

ADDITIONAL SIGHTSEEING

Look up Matthew 6:19-21, Psalm 62:10, Luke 12:15, and Proverbs 11:28

What warnings do you see about riches on earth? (Answers on bottom)

Matthew 6:19-21

Psalm 62:10

Luke 12:15

Proverbs 11:28

1. Riches on earth will eventually be destroyed. Riches in heaven will never be destroyed. 2. Even though your wealth increases, do not put your hope in them. 3. A man's life is not valued by how rich he is. 4. Do not trust in riches, trust in GOD.

STOP
and write down your prayers.

Lord,

Please help me to remember that material possessions on this earth are temporary. You intended them for our pleasure, NOT as a place in which to put our hope. I pray to not be self-indulgent but to always TRUST in YOU.

Amen.

James 5:1-6

JAMES 5:7-11

10-MINUTE OIL CHANGE

"Be patient, then, brothers and sisters, until the Lord's coming. See how the farmer waits for the land to yield its valuable crop, patiently waiting for the autumn and spring rains. You too, be **patient** and stand firm, because the Lord's coming is near. Don't grumble against one another, brothers and sisters, or you will be judged. The Judge is standing at the door! Brothers and sisters, as an example of patience in the face of suffering, take the prophets who spoke in the name of the Lord. As you know, we count as blessed those who have persevered. You have heard of Job's perseverance and have seen what the Lord finally brought about. The Lord is full of compassion and mercy."

DEFINITION: Patient

1. able to wait without becoming annoyed or anxious

DISCUSSION

This verse can be challenging in a world that teaches us that we do not have to wait long for anything! Think about it—your FOOD is fast, and your Internet is fast. You have instant text messaging, email, digital photography, and 10-minute oil changes. Why wait when you can get something RIGHT now? James is reminding us in this passage that perseverance and patience is very important when standing firm through difficult circumstances. WHY? It's simple. The PROMISE that Jesus IS coming back. When Jesus ascended into heaven after His crucifixion, death, and resurrection, He promised us He would return again!

Madison didn't want to wait any longer. The science project was due tomorrow and she didn't have time to wait for paint to dry. The directions said to let the first coat dry overnight before adding the second coat, but maybe 10-minutes was good enough. Madison knew she needed to speed things up. In haste, she quickly applied the second coat of paint to her science project. But quicker than her five-minute presentation, the first coat of paint buckled up. Why couldn't she wait? Why did she always have to rush things? Her project was ruined. Her only hope at this point was praying her science teacher would have some compassion.

Why is it so hard to wait? Madison's science project is a simple example for a tough question. We have learned in James that patience builds maturity of faith, completeness in character, and provision of blessing. Yes, Jesus is returning. Are you patient enough to wait?

DIRECTIONAL QUESTIONS

1. What has been hard to wait for in your life?

2. What two examples of patience are given in this passage? Why do you think they persevered?

3. What are we told NOT to do during the waiting time? Why do you think this is important?

4. What is PROMISED in this passage? Why is this important?

"LORD GIVE ME PATIENCE, BUT HURRY!"

BACKROAD DRIVIN'

It's important to remember Jesus' PROMISE that He IS coming back again. It is also IMPORTANT to know that when He left, He did not leave us alone. Jesus left us with the Holy Spirit to teach us, remind us, and counsel us to **Follow God's Road Signs.** Yes, it is hard to be patient and persevere when we are suffering, but Jesus never intended that we suffer alone. Job is a great example to remind us to endure under extremely difficult circumstances. He lost his family, his livestock, and his health. While his friends, and even his own wife, encouraged him to curse God and die— he chose the road that led to life. He CHOSE to believe that GOD had a better plan, even when life seemed like absolute darkness. Because of Job's perseverance, he was considered BLESSED by God. Galatians 6:9 tells us, "not to become weary in doing good, for we WILL reap a harvest if we do not give up." Just like the farmer and just like Job, we must NOT become tired of doing what's right, even when we are pushed to our limit. We will see Jesus face-to-face one day.

ADDITIONAL SIGHTSEEING

Look up Romans 8:17-18, Titus 2:12-14, and 2 Corinthians 4:16-18

How are we supposed to WAIT for the LORD? (Answers on bottom)

Romans 8:17-18

Titus 2:12-14

2 Corinthians 4:16-18

1. We are to wait as CHILDREN of the Lord. Our present sufferings are not worth comparing to the glory of Christ. 2. We are to wait with Godly lives. 3. We are to wait with our eyes FIXED on Jesus and not on this world - which is temporary.

STOP
and write down your prayers.

Lord,

I know You are FULL of compassion and mercy. I pray this week to be more patient. I pray also to not give up when life gets hard, but to call upon Your Holy Spirit to guide me and direct me in the way I should go. Thank You Jesus for not leaving me alone!

Amen.

James 5:7-11

JAMES 5:12-16

CLEAN OUT YOUR CAR

"Above all, my brothers, do not swear—not by heaven or by earth or by anything else. Let your 'Yes' be yes, and your 'No,' no, or you will be condemned. Is any one of you in trouble? He should pray. Is anyone happy? Let him sing songs of praise. Is any one of you sick? He should call the elders of the church to pray over him and anoint him with oil in the name of the Lord. And the prayer offered in faith will make the sick person well; the Lord will raise him up. If he has sinned, he will be forgiven. Therefore **confess** your sins to each other and pray for each other so that you may be healed. The prayer of a righteous man is powerful and effective."

DEFINITION: Confess

1. to make an acknowledgment or admission of faults, or misdeeds

DISCUSSION

James begins this verse with another serious announcement. You can almost hear his voice becoming louder and stronger as we come to his closing statements. "ABOVE ALL," he begins, "Let your 'yes' be yes and your 'no' be no." Can you list the actions we have studied in chapter five that fall underneath this **above all** statement? We have looked at not falling into the money trap and returning things that belong to others (5:1-5). We have looked at being patient, waiting for the Lord's return, standing firm, and not grumbling (5:6-11). Here we see, above ALL, our word takes precedent. And when we keep it, God is highly exalted.

Rose was so excited, she could hardly breathe. Colin had just invited her to the Spring dance. She rushed to her calendar when her eyes landed on April 4th. "No, it's not THAT night," she whispered under her breath. Rose's heart sank. She had already committed to volunteer for the "Special Needs" Prom. And when Rose said "Yes" to something, she was good for her word. She had always taken pride in that . . . until today. "Maybe they won't need me. After all, I am just a volunteer," she thought. Rose began to text her coordinator when her Mom walked in to her room. After telling her Mom what happened and praying about the situation, she knew exactly what she had to do. Rose reached for her phone and began dialing Colin's number.

It's hard to keep your word when you REALLY want to do something else. But God makes it clear, our "yes" means yes and our "no" means no, even when another opportunity looks better. This is a true testimony of FAITH in our journey of **Following His Road Signs**.

DIRECTIONAL QUESTIONS

1. When has your "YES" meant YES, and your "NO" meant NO? Have you ever been in a situation like Maggie?

2. What are the four action verbs in these verses? What circumstances make you USE these verbs? Do you?

3. Why do you think it is important to confess your sins BEFORE you pray?

4. Have you ever experienced a powerful prayer? Tell us about it.

"LET YOUR YES BE YES AND YOUR NO BE NO" -JAMES

BACKROAD DRIVIN'

CLEAN out your car! James tells us to **confess** our sins. Have you done this lately? We all pray, right? But is your heart clean BEFORE you say, "yes" or "no" to something... before you PRAY, SING, CALL, or CONFESS? James tells us that there is POWER in prayer. However, in order for your prayers to be effective... you need to make sure your HEART is in the right place. This is not new to us, since we have studied the entire book of James! (Great job, by the way.) In chapter two, we saw that our faith and actions begin with a heart that desires to please God. In chapter three, we saw that our speech and wisdom also begins with a pure heart to serve our Lord. In chapter four, we found that God knows our heart and can see our true motives, whether it is in the asking or the planning. Remember this verse from Luke 6:45?

> "The good man brings good things out of the good stored up in his heart, and the evil man brings evil things out of the evil stored up in his heart. For out of the overflow of his heart his mouth speaks."

Our cars need to be clean and our hearts do, too! Confess your sins to one another so your prayers can be POWERFUL and EFFECTIVE.

ADDITIONAL SIGHTSEEING

Look up Psalm 97:9, Ephesians 1:19-23, 1 Peter 4:8, Col. 3:12-14, and 2 Peter 1:20-21

There are many ABOVE ALL statements in Scripture! What are they? (Answers on bottom)

Psalm 97:9

Ephesians 1:19-23

1 Peter 4:8

Col. 3:12-14

2 Peter 1:20-21

1. GOD is above all. 2. Jesus is above all. 3. Love is above all. 4. Love binds all virtues. 5. Above all, we must understand that Scripture is from GOD, not man.

STOP and write down your prayers.

Lord,

I pray my word is true before YOU and others. I also pray to clean out my heart so I can PRAISE You with song and seek You when I am in trouble or sick. Thank You for the promise that prayer is powerful and effective.

Amen.

James 5:12-16

JAMES 5:17-20

U-TURN AHEAD

"Elijah was a human being, even as we are. He prayed earnestly that it would not rain, and it did not rain on the land for three and a half years. Again he prayed, and the heavens gave rain, and the earth produced its crops. My brothers and sisters, if one of you should **wander** from the truth and someone should bring that person back, remember this: Whoever turns a sinner from the error of their way will save them from death and cover over a multitude of sins."

DEFINITION: Wander

1. walk or move in a leisurely, casual, or aimless way
2. to move about without a definite destination or purpose

DISCUSSION

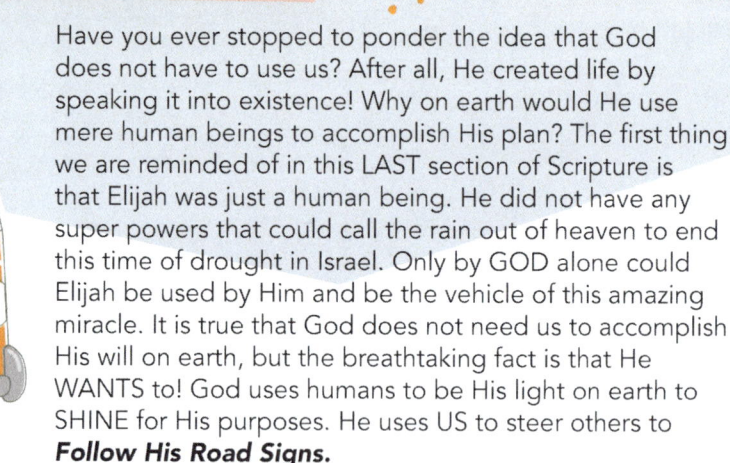

Have you ever stopped to ponder the idea that God does not have to use us? After all, He created life by speaking it into existence! Why on earth would He use mere human beings to accomplish His plan? The first thing we are reminded of in this LAST section of Scripture is that Elijah was just a human being. He did not have any super powers that could call the rain out of heaven to end this time of drought in Israel. Only by GOD alone could Elijah be used by Him and be the vehicle of this amazing miracle. It is true that God does not need us to accomplish His will on earth, but the breathtaking fact is that He WANTS to! God uses humans to be His light on earth to SHINE for His purposes. He uses US to steer others to **Follow His Road Signs.**

"Yes, Lord, I want to be a TESTimony for you. But, I had no idea how hard the test would be!" Being a Christian is hard. My friends think I'm weird going to a Bible Study and not being absolutely boy crazy. I really hate the drama about which friend group you are in, what you are wearing to the game, where you live, what phone you have, and what your parents do for a living. Lord, does all this really matter? My best friend seems to be buying into all these games. Lord, help *me point her back to you. I pray You will give me the words that make sense. Only YOU can satisfy her hunger for life. You are the giver of perfect gifts—not the world. I am learning that the things of this world do NOT satisfy and are only temporary. Kind of like highschool! Ha! Thank you Lord! ~ Hallie's Journal*

To **wander** is to move without destination or purpose. This is the opposite of **Following God's Road Signs**. Being a testimony can be quite a test! Regardless of the difficulty, we have God on our side. Let's choose to be used by Him!

DIRECTIONAL QUESTIONS

1. Why does God choose to use humans to accomplish His purposes?

2. What role does prayer have in God's purposes? (Think back to last lesson.)

3. Where do you feel following God's plan for your life is challenging?

4. Have you ever lost sight of **Following God's Road Signs** or helped someone to get back on track?

"GOD ALLOWS U-TURNS!"

BACKROAD DRIVIN'

Elijah was in a TESTing situation! Why would James recall this story to close his letter? During this time in history, the Israelites were worshiping false gods. Not only was their land in shortage of water, but their hearts were in shortage for the ONE and TRUE GOD. God chose to use Elijah, a prophet, to display His power, authority, and might. God allowed Elijah to be His earthly vehicle to PRAY for rain. And at Elijah's command, it rained and it stopped. It's an amazing story found in 1 Kings 17. Today, we also experience dry times in our lives that are in some need of God-rain! When we put certain "things" before our relationship with God, we, too, are worshiping false gods. We might put friends, boys, appearance, social media, relationships, clothes, etc . . . before God. These worldly things block our vision of God causing us to put more value on the temporary. James is abruptly closing his letter by saying, "NO!" **Your salvation in Jesus is the only thing that matters!** Do not lose sight of this. And if you see your friend falling away from Jesus, bring her back. It can be easy to follow the ways of the world, especially when they seem like so much fun. But, BE AWARE, call on God to draw near, and take the U-turn that leads to life.

ADDITIONAL SIGHTSEEING

Look up 1 Peter 3:15, Mark 16:15, 2 Timothy 1:8-12, and John 10:27-30.

You are called to be a witness for Jesus. His sacrifice covers your multitude of sins. How are you to do this? (Answers on bottom)

1 Peter 3:15

Mark 16:15

2 Timothy 1:8-12

John 10:27-30

1. We need to be prepared to talk about our faith with gentleness and respect. 2. We are called to GO and proclaim. 3. We are not to be ashamed but convinced. 4. We have to believe that Jesus gives eternal life.

STOP
and write down your prayers.

Lord,

You are an amazing GOD! Just the fact alone that You CHOOSE to use me is beyond belief. I want to be used by You. Give me the wisdom, guidance, and words to not only live my life for You, but also help those who are wandering.

Amen.

James 5:17-20

JAMES 5:1-20

Artist Workshop Ahead

THE HOUSE OF GOD

"The prayer of a righteous person is powerful and effective." James 5:16

THE HOUSE of God

HOW TO:

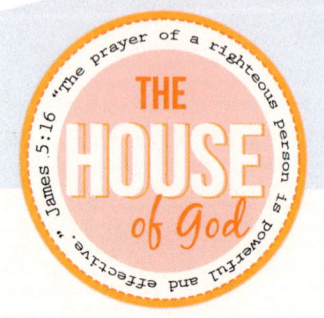

1. Have two 2x4's cut to size: one for the roof and one for the house. The size of your house doesn't matter. It could be tall like the one photographed or smaller like one in the video.

2. Sand your wood and paint the house and the roof.

3. While drying, cut soda can (see video).

4. Using the roof as a template, trace the triangle shape onto the back side of the can with a sharpie. Cut out and tack triangle onto roof.

5. Hammer tacks to secure aluminum to roof. Now you have a tin roof!

6. There are MANY ways to decorate your house. The video shows two options. One: Using a wooden clip, clip a picture of the person you are praying for. Two: Use fabric to wrap your house and slip your picture in the fabric. The picture on pg. 119 shows a door knob symbolizing the House of God is always open for prayer.

7. Download and print templates. Embellish your house with scrapbook paper, yarn, wire, etc.

8. Glue roof and house together using wood glue.

9. Using two sticks, glue the cross together and reinforce with wire or twine. Glue cross to the roof.

ART STOP

ART SUPPLIES:

- 2 x 4's: 2 pieces
- Roof: Cut at a Slant
- House: 7-8 Inches Height (this can vary)
- Glue Sticks
- Low Temp Hot Glue Gun
- Scrapbooking Paper
- Sharpie
- Ribbon, Wire, Yarn, Cording, Trim, Etc.
- Embellishments (Buttons, Sequins, wire, etc.)
- Printer and Cardstock Paper
- Scissors
- Wood Glue
- Hammer
- Tacks
- Soda Can
- Paint
- Sand Paper
- Wooden Clip
- Door Knob (optional)

DOWNLOAD THE HOUSE OF GOD and TEMPLATES
@ thouartexalted.com/James-art

This is the password:
GREEN LIGHT

- **Chapter Five Review:** Be patient and STAND FIRM for the Lord's coming. Do not grumble. The Lord is FULL of compassion and mercy. Do not swear. Let your YES be YES and your NO be NO. When you are in trouble, pray. When you are happy, praise Him. When you are sick, PRAY, and confess your sins to each other. The PRAYER of a RIGHTEOUS man is POWERFUL and EFFECTIVE. If someone has wandered from the truth, bring them back.

Your prayers are effective. The House of God art project will be a reminder to ask for God's direction and pray. Add a picture of the person you are praying for and clip it to your house. Be patient and remember the Lord is full of compassion and mercy.

JAMES Chapter 1-5

THE ROAD OF REVIEW

THANKSGIVING & PRAYER
Philippians 1:3-6, 9-11

"I THANK my God every time I remember you. In all my prayers for all of you, I always pray with JOY because of your partnership in the gospel from the first day until now, being confident of this, that He who began a good work in you will carry it on to completion until the day of Christ Jesus."

"And this is my prayer: that your love may abound more and more in knowledge and depth of insight, so that you may be able to discern what is best and may be pure and blameless for the day of Christ, filled with the fruit of righteousness that comes through Jesus Christ—to the glory and praise of God."

REVIEW

Congratulations! You did it! You have studied the WHOLE book of James. And if you chose to do the art components, you will have completed five projects that will help you to remember the study. **Following God's Road Signs** will always be available if you have your art displayed in a prominent place.

Let's take a quick trip down the **Road of Review.** We will go through each chapter and highlight the Road Signs.

- **Chapter One:** Consider it JOY when you go through many trials. Perseverance builds maturity. Every GOOD and PERFECT gift is from above. Be quick to listen, slow to speak, and slow to become angry. Do not merely listen to the word, but do what it SAYS. Keep yourself from being polluted by this world.

- **Chapter Two:** Don't show Favoritism. Love your neighbor as yourself. Mercy TRIUMPHS over judgment. Faith without action is DEAD.

- **Chapter Three:** Don't presume to be a teacher because those who teach will be judged more strictly. The tongue is a small part of the body, but it makes great boasts. We praise the Father and curse men. Wisdom is two-fold: Earthly and Godly. Earthly wisdom is full of disorder and evil. Godly wisdom is pure, peace-loving, considerate, submissive, full of mercy, good fruit, impartial, and sincere. Peacemakers will sow a harvest of righteousness.

- **Chapter Four:** Fights and quarrels come from the desires within you. You do not have because you do not ask. Ask with the right motives. A friend of this world is an enemy of God. God gives MORE GRACE. Submit to God and resist the devil. Come NEAR to GOD and He will come NEAR to you. Humble yourselves before the Lord and He WILL lift you up. There is only ONE Judge. Do not boast about tomorrow. Instead, ASK God to reveal His will.

- **Chapter Five:** Be patient and STAND FIRM for the Lord's coming. Do not grumble. The Lord is FULL of compassion and mercy. Do not swear. Let your YES be YES and your NO be NO. When you are in trouble, pray. When you are happy, praise Him. When you are sick, PRAY, and confess your sins to each other. The PRAYER of a RIGHTEOUS man is POWERFUL and EFFECTIVE. If someone has wandered from the truth, bring them back.

DIRECTIONAL QUESTIONS

1. Looking back at each chapter, what lesson meant the most to you?

2. What did you like best about this study?

3. Going forward, how are you going to **Follow God's Road Signs?**

"I THANK MY GOD EVERY TIME I THINK OF YOU..."

My prayer for YOU comes from Philippians 1:3-6, 9-11.

I DO thank GOD for ALL of you! I celebrate with JOY because you have persevered to FINISH this study! I am confident that God, who began a GOOD work in you, will carry it on to completion throughout the rest of your lives. I pray also that the Scripture we learned together will continue to grow in your hearts so that you can use this treasure of knowledge and wisdom when you need it the most. I pray you will continue to follow Jesus and rely on Him and not the world to lead you in the right direction. **Following GOD's Road Signs** will allow you to discern what is BEST~ all to the glory and PRAISE of God.

May His blessings rest on each and every one of you.

ALL my love,
ANNIE

STOP and write down your prayers.

Lord,

Thank YOU that I finished this Bible Study on James, **Following God's Road Signs.** I pray to make good choices that will steer me on the right road and take me in the right direction. Thank You for James and for writing this book. May I always look to Your wisdom to follow YOU.

Amen.

#IFOLLOWGODSROADSIGNS

JAMES 5:7-20

Artist Workshop Ahead

THE JAMES JOURNAL

Bonus Art Project!

HOW TO:

...Come near to God and he will come near to you. James 4:8

THE JAMES journal

1. Print out the James Journal template found under the James Journal Art Instructions and Video.

2. Using your composition book as a template, trace the open booklet onto your wallpaper or scrapbook paper. Tip: Use two coordinating papers for the front back. If you choose to do this, wrap the back of the book 2 inches into the front cover to make a "spine." (see video)

3. Cut out and glue paper to the outside of your composition book. Tip: Use a credit card to scrape away any air bubbles.

4. Cut out the bus, graphics, and Scripture and glue to your cover with a glud stick.

5. Add ribbon, buttons, and glitter to your journal.

6. Now you have a place to write down and journal all that you have learned in **James: Following God's Road Signs!**

ART STOP

Jesus loves you

ART SUPPLIES:

- Composition Book
- Wallpaper or Scrapbook Paper
- Glue or Modge Podge
- Optional Low-Temp Hot Glue Gun
- Glue Sticks
- Ribbon or Yarn
- Pencil
- One Inch Foam Brush
- Scissors
- Embellishments (Buttons, Sequins, Glitter, etc.)
- Printer and Paper
- Templates
- Credit Card

DOWNLOAD THE JAMES JOURNAL VIDEO and TEMPLATES @ **thouartexalted.com/James-art**

This is the password:
GREEN LIGHT

YOU DID IT! The James Journal is an EXTRA art project in our study of **James: Following God's Road Signs.** Journaling is a great way to write down the lessons God is teaching you to remember HIS FAITHFULNESS. God doesn't care about spelling or grammar. He just wants you to write down what He is pressing on your heart. Are you ready? Get your paper, composition book, and glue. Let's get started!

MORE STUDIES FOR TWEEN AND TEEN GIRLS!

AWAKE MY SOUL DEVOTIONAL

Did you know there are 260 days in a week (Monday-Friday) and 260 chapters in the New Testament? Authored by over 55 women and girls, Awake My Soul is the perfect devotional for tween and teen girls to read through the New Testament in ONE YEAR!

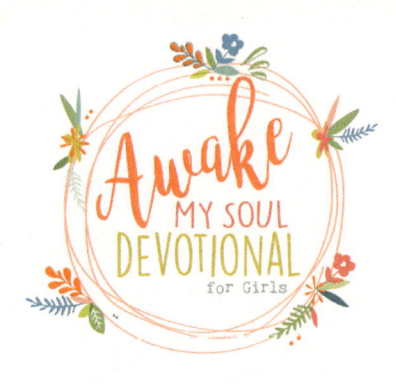

260 New Testament Devotions
By ThouArtExalted Ministries

Riding Tandem

Riding Tandem/Leaning into the Leading of God for tween and teen girls is a 12-week Bible study filled with art, fun, and surprises! It's about an authentic, one-on-one relationship with God. It's about learning our position on the back of the bike and trusting God with the front steering. Our personal relationship with God is built for two. He is the Captain and we must learn to lean into His leading, pedal forward, and trust Him with the directions.

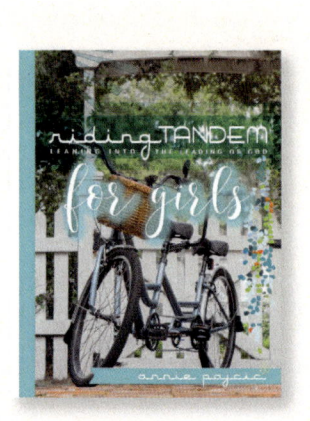

FIVE-Small Group Series

FIVE is a creative, five-week study for tween and teen girls featuring five lessons and one art project. Studies include:

- A Seed To Sow
- Brave
- Love is ALL you Need
- Project 2911
- The In and Out Cafe: Jealousy is NOT on the Menu
- The Perfect Present

TAE BIBLE STUDIES

HE KNOWS MY NAME
20/20 Mini-Lessons

He Knows My Name 20/20 Mini-Lessons for Girls is a creative Biblical study for middle school girls **ages 10-14**. Based on John 10:3, the Good Shepherd calls His sheep by name and leads them out. Jesus is our Good Shepherd and we, His children, are the sheep of His pasture. Using the imagery of sheep and shepherds, He Knows My Name teaches girls that God will always love, protect, and lead to safe pastures. This study also includes five art projects.

Annie Pajcic

Annie lives in Jacksonville, Florida with her husband and four children. Using her background in youth ministry, art, and graphic design, she started `ThouArtExalted` in 2007. ThouArtExalted is a non-profit 501(c)(3) ministry inspiring women and girls to live creatively for Christ. When Annie doesn't have paint on her hands, she is writing, designing, teaching Bible studies, going to lacrosse tournaments, cooking dinner, or feeding the chickens. Visit her website at **www.thouartexalted.com** for speaking engagements, art ideas, Bible studies, special events, and devotionals.

Made in the USA
Columbia, SC
04 March 2021